An Anthology

OF PIECES FROM EARLY EDITIONS OF

ENCYCLOPÆDIA BRITANNICA

ENCYCLOPÆDIA BRITANNICA LTD
LONDON

The extracts chosen for this anthology have been taken from articles in editions published during the first 100 years of the ENCYCLOPÆDIA BRITANNICA'S *continuous existence, that is, from the first edition of 1768–71 to the eighth of 1853–60 (there are no selections from the fifth and sixth, which were revised and corrected reprints). Spelling and punctuation have been reproduced unchanged; . . . indicates omitted matter except where so insignificant as to warrant silent change.*

PRINTED IN GREAT BRITAIN

INTRODUCTION

THE EDITOR of the first edition (1768–71) of the *Encyclopaedia Britannica*, William Smellie, begins his preface with a bold declaration of purpose: "Utility ought to be the principal intention of every publication. Wherever this intention does not plainly appear, neither the books nor their authors have the smallest claim to the approbation of mankind." The sweeping proposition is true enough of the encyclopaedic class of publication that Smellie had in mind; and, from the first edition published nearly 200 years ago, successive issues of *Britannica* have tried to make an ordered range of information, the concentrated essence of a fair-sized library, easily accessible, in accordance with his ideal.

At the same time each edition has represented the state of knowledge and the opinions of its own age; and the reader scanning these earlier pages may become absorbed by the picture they give of the beliefs and attitudes, insights and misconceptions, and bygone activities of their day. The pieces in this anthology offer, often lightheartedly, just such a reflection of a past age and its interests; not, let it be said, the addition of superseded and occasionally erroneous instruction to the current printing of *Britannica*.

The anthology covers a period when the Napoleonic Wars followed the loss of the American colonies; the Industrial Revolution in full stride brought stirrings of social change, agitation for reform and labour unrest; the Romantic view came to prevail in the arts; steam and iron conquered space and time with steamship and railway. Our own wonder at the Russian and American astronautical feats is anticipated by excitement at the perilous heights attained in early balloon ascents and by amazement at the triumph of George Stephenson's locomotive. Some of these things are reflected in the extracts, together with many obscurer matters now forgotten. Development of thought is less even and less rapid than scientific progress, and assumptions of the literal truth of the Book of Genesis retain a place beside the Benthamite ideas of James Mill and T. R. Malthus.

Till the publication of the supplement to the fourth, fifth and sixth editions, contributions had been unsigned, but in that work the successful policy of inviting contributions from the most eminent authorities resulted in the signing of major articles henceforth, and authors of such extracts are therefore named in the anthology and a word or two of description of them is given. The anthology includes, from this supplement, James Mill on education, government, prison and the liberty of the press, Francis Jeffrey on beauty, Sir John Leslie on aeronautics, J. R. McCullough on political economy, taxation and combination by workpeople, T. R. Malthus on population, John Playfair on the progress of science, David Ricardo on the funding system, P. M. Roget on cranioscopy, Sir Walter Scott on chivalry, Dugald Stewart on the progress of philosophy, John Bird Sumner, later archbishop of Canterbury, on the poor laws and Thomas Young on the Rosetta stone; from the seventh and eighth editions, Charles Apperley ("Nimrod") on hunting, Walter Bagehot on the Crédit Mobilier, Thomas De Quincey, B. R. Haydon, William Hazlitt, Charles Kingsley and Lord Macaulay on subjects of literature and art, Robert Stephenson on bridges, James Watt on steam, Moderator David Welsh on Jesus Christ and Archbishop Whately on the progress of Christianity.

In his preface to the seventh edition, the editor, Macvey Napier, glances at the encyclopaedia's progress over 70 years with a proud, if unloyal, boast: "The workmanship, at first, of a few comparatively undistinguished literary denizens of its native place; its list of contributors now includes a large portion of that learned host by whom the mental sovereignty of Britain is upheld." The inclination to disparage the first steps is no longer felt from the vantage point of historical distance: youth may reject childhood but mature age acknowledges it gratefully. In fact, the *Encyclopaedia Britannica* is probably fortunate to have been born in Edinburgh, where solid scholarship and humane rationalism provided as fair a climate as any in which to nurture such an enterprise. It is evident that the great work struck out strongly enough nearly 200 years ago.

NOTE ON EDITIONS

The *Encyclopaedia Britannica* was the project of Andrew Bell and Colin Macfarquhar, an engraver and a printer respectively, of Edinburgh and was subscribed for by a "society of gentlemen in Scotland";

under the editorship of William Smellie, the first edition began to appear in weekly 6*d.* numbers in Dec. 1768, publication being completed in 1771, in three volumes containing 2,659 pages.

Smellie, who became secretary and superintendent of natural history to the Society of Scottish Antiquaries, refused to undertake a second edition at Bell's request because he disapproved of the scheme to include biographies. Instead James Tytler, a self-taught but considerable scholar, whose passionate interest in balloon ascents won him the nickname of "balloon" Tytler, was chosen to edit the second edition which, issued in 181 numbers from June 21, 1777, was completed in 1783, in ten volumes, containing 8,595 pages and 340 plates. The plan of the work was enlarged by the addition of history and biography.

The third edition was edited by Macfarquhar till his death in 1793 and then by George Gleig, later bishop of Brechin, and appeared in numbers from 1788 to its completion in 1797, in 18 volumes containing 14,579 pages and 542 plates. Bell now purchased Macfarquhar's share in the copyright and stock of the encyclopaedia from his heirs. A two-volume supplement to the third edition, edited by Gleig, was published in 1801 (1,624 pages and 50 plates).

The fourth edition, edited by Dr. James Millar, was begun in 1800 and finished in 1810, in 20 volumes containing 16,033 pages and 581 plates. In 1804 Bell had offered the copyright and what was then printed of the fourth edition to the Edinburgh bookseller and publisher Archibald Constable; after Bell's death in 1809 and the mismanagement of the fifth edition, little more than a reprint of the fourth, by Bell's trustees, Constable bought the encyclopaedia. The fifth edition was published by 1817, in 20 volumes, the last 15 of which Millar corrected and revised. The sixth edition,

a revision and correction of the fifth, was published in half-volumes from 1820 and was completed in May 1823, mainly under the editorship of Charles Maclaren.

Meanwhile Constable had prepared for the publication of a supplement, and its editorship was entrusted to Macvey Napier, who had assisted Gleig with the third edition and himself was now of some account in the world of letters. The supplement to the fourth, fifth and sixth editions—its publication overlapped the issue of the two latter editions—appeared from Dec. 1816 to April 1824, in six volumes containing 4,933 pages, 125 plates and 9 maps. It was a landmark in that contributions were obtained, thanks to the energy of Napier and his encouragement by Constable, from great authorities of the day, and these contributions included three prefatory, major dissertations on progress in the fields of science and philosophy.

A new edition was contemplated, but Constable's house failed in 1826 and Adam Black, another Edinburgh bookseller and publisher, and his partners bought the copyright in 1828, Black later buying out his partners and bringing a relative, Charles, in with him. The seventh edition was edited by Napier and was published from March 1830 to Jan. 1842, in 21 volumes (with a 187-page index) containing 17,101 pages, 507 plates and the dissertations from the supplement.

The eighth edition was edited (Napier having died in 1847) by Thomas Stewart Traill, professor of medical jurisprudence in Edinburgh university, and was published from 1853 to 1860, in 21 volumes (239-page index, 1861) containing 17,957 pages and 402 plates. Added to the previous dissertations was a historical survey of Christianity by Archbishop Richard Whately.

A.A.A. A Man, Woman, & Child of Easter Island.
B. Woman of New Zeeland.
C. A New Zeeland Warrior.
D. Native of New Caledonia.
E. Woman of New Holland.
F. Woman of O-Taheitee.
G. Another Woman of O-Taheitee with a Bonnet of Leaves.
H. A Man of O-Taheitee.
I. A Man of Mallicollo.
K.K. A Man & Woman of S.t Christina, in the Marquesas.
L. A Priest of the Society Islands.
M. Dancing Girl at Ulietea.
N. A Musician playing on a Lute from his Nose.
O. The Drum of Ulietea.
P. A Bier & the manner of depositing the Dead at the Society Isld.s
Q. Habit of Mourning at O-Taheitee.
R. A Canoe of the Friendly Isl.s
S. A Fortified Village of N. Zeeland.
T. A Canoe of O-Taheitee.
U. A Branch of the Bread Fruit Tree, with the Fruit.
W. The Kanguroo, an Animal
peculiar to New Holland.
X. The manner of constructing Houses at O-Taheitee.
Y. A Species of the Fig Tree found in New Caledonia.
Z. A Floating Ice Island, numbers of which were seen towards the Southern Frigid Zone.

A. Bell Sculp.t

From the second edition (1777–83).

Mr. Baldwin's Ascent from Chester

On the 8th of September 1785, at forty minutes past one P.M. Mr. Baldwin ascended from Chester in Mr. Lunardi's balloon. After traversing in a variety of different directions, he first alighted, at 28 minutes after three, about twelve miles from Chester, in the neighbourhood of Frodsham; then reascending and pursuing his excursion, he finally landed at Rixtonmoss, five miles N.N.E. of Warrington, and 25 miles from Chester. Our limits will not admit of relating many of his observations; but the few following are some of the most important and curious. The sensation of ascending is compared to that of a strong pressure from the bottom of the car upwards against the soles of his feet. At the distance of what appeared to him seven miles from the earth, though by the barometer scarcely a mile and a half, he had a grand and most enchanting view of the city of Chester and its adjacent places below. The river Dee appeared of a red colour; the city very diminutive; and the town entirely blue. The whole appeared a perfect plain, the highest building having no apparent height, but reduced all to the same level, and the whole terrestrial prospect appeared like a coloured map. Just after his first ascent, being in a well-watered and maritime part of the country, he observed a remarkable and regular tendency of the balloon towards the sea; but shortly after rising into another current of air, he escaped the danger: this upper current, he says, was visible to him at the time of his ascent, by a lofty sound stratum of clouds flying in a safe direction. The perspective appearance of things to him was very remarkable. The lowest bed of vapour that first appeared as cloud was pure white, in detached fleeces, increasing as they rose: they presently coalesced, and formed, as he expresses it, a sea of cotton, tufting here and there by the action of the air in the undisturbed part of the clouds. The whole became an extended white floor of cloud, the upper surface being smooth and even. Above this white floor he observed, at great and unequal distances, a vast assemblage of thunder-clouds, each parcel consisting of whole acres in the densest form: he compares their form and appearance to the smoke of pieces of ordnance, which had consolidated as it were into masses of snow, and penetrated through the upper surface or white floor of common clouds, there remaining visible and at rest. Some clouds had motions in slow and various directions, forming an appearance truly stupendous and majestic. Mr. Baldwin also gives a curious description of his tracing the shadow of the balloon over tops of volumes of clouds. At first it was small, in size and shape like an egg; but soon increased to the magnitude of the sun's disc, still growing larger, and attended with a most captivating appearance of an iris encircling the whole shadow at some distance round it, the colours of which were remarkably brilliant. The regions did not feel colder, but rather warmer, than below. The sun was hottest to him when the balloon was stationary. The discharge of a cannon when the balloon was at considerable height, was distinctly heard by the aeronaut; and a discharge from the same piece, when at the height of 30 yards, so disturbed him as to oblige him for safety to lay hold firmly of the cords of the balloon. At a considerable height he poured down a pint-bottle full of water; and as the air did not oppose a resistance sufficient to break the steam into small drops, it mostly fell down in large drops. In the course of the balloon's tract it was found much affected by the water (a circumstance observed in former aerial voyages). At one time the direction of the balloon kept continually over the water, going directly towards the sea, so much as to endanger the aeronaut; the mouth of the balloon was opened and he in two minutes descended into an under current blowing from the sea: he kept descending, and landed at Bellair farm in Rinsley, 12 miles from Chester. Here he lightened his car by 31 pounds, and instantly reascending, was carried into the interior part of the country, performing a number of different manœuvres. At his greatest altitude he found his respiration free and easy. Several bladders which he had along with him crackled and expanded very considerably. Clouds and land, as before, appeared on the same level. By way

of experiment, he tried the upper valve two or three times, the neck of the balloon being close; and remarked, that the escape of the gas was attended with a growling noise like millstones, but not near so loud. Again, round the shadow of the balloon, on the clouds he observed the iris. A variety of other circumstances and appearances he met with, is fancifully described; and at 53 minutes past three he finally landed.

AEROSTATION, third edition (1788–97).

A Cumberland Cloudscape

From the tops of the mountains in Cumberland, the views are alike extensive and varied. The summit of Skiddaw brings under the eye the Irish Sea and the German Ocean,—a chaos of dark mountains at a distance, with lakes seen dimly at the feet of the nearest, and a vast expanse of champaign country, bounded by the Irish Channel, and traversed by silvery thread-like streams in every direction. Upon the summits of the Cross-fell ridge, there frequently hangs a vast volume of clouds, reaching half way down to the base of the fells. At some distance from this *helm*, as it is called, and opposite to it, another cloud called the *helm-bar*, is seen in continual agitation, while the helm itself remains motionless. When the *bar* is dispersed, the wind rushes from the helm, often with great fury, and sometimes on both sides of the mountains.

CUMBERLAND, supplement to the fourth, fifth and sixth editions (1816–24).

Aeronautics

Navigation, in its most cultivated form, may be fairly regarded as the consummation of art, and the sublimest triumph of human genius, industry, courage, and perseverance.

Having by his skill achieved the conquest of the waters that encompass the habitable globe, it was natural for man to desire likewise the mastery of the air in which we breathe. In all ages, accordingly, has ingenuity been tortured in vain efforts at flying. The story of Icarus testifies how fatal such daring attempts had generally proved to their projectors.

The scheme of flying in the air, which men of the first genius had once entertained, appears to have gradually descended to a lower class of projectors. Those who afterwards occupied themselves with such hopeless at-

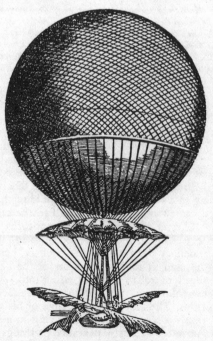

Blanchard's balloon. From AEROSTATION, *third edition* (1788–97).

tempts, had commonly a smattering of mechanics, with some little share of ingenuity, but wrought up by excessive conceit.

The practice of aëronautics has not realized those expectations of benefit to mankind which sanguine projectors were at first disposed to entertain. It was soon found, that a balloon, launched into the atmosphere, is abandoned, without guidance or command, to the mercy of the winds. To undertake to direct or impel the floating machine by any exertion of human strength, was evidently a chimerical attempt. All the influence which the aëronaut really possesses consists in a very limited power of raising or depressing it, according to circumstances. He cannot hope to shape his course, unless by skilfully adapting his elevation to catch the prevailing currents.

Almost the only purpose to which balloons have hitherto been applied with success, had for its object that of military *reconnoissance*. In the early part of the French revolutionary war, when ingenuity and science were so eagerly called into active service, a balloon, prepared under the direction of the *Aërostatic Institute* in the Polytechnic School, and intrusted to the command of two or three experienced officers, was distributed to each of the republican armies. The decisive victory which General Jourdan gained, in June 1794, over the Austrian forces in the plains of Fleurus, has been ascribed principally to the accurate information of the enemy's movements before and during the battle, communicated by telegraphical signals from a balloon which was sent up to a moderate height in the air.

The ascents with balloons should appear to furnish the readiest means of ascertaining important facts in meteorology and atmospheric electricity, departments of science which are still unfortunately in their infancy. A few years since [1804], two young and ardent French philosophers, MM. Biot and Gay-Lussac, proposed to undertake an aërial ascent, in order to examine the magnetic force at great elevations, and to explore the constitution of the higher atmosphere and its electrical properties.

The ascents performed by MM. Biot and Gay-Lussac are memorable, for being the first ever undertaken solely for objects of science. It is impossible not to admire the intrepid coolness with which they conducted those experiments, operating, while they floated in the highest regions of the atmosphere, with the same

Montgolfier's Versailles balloon. From AEROSTATION, *third ed.* (1788–97).

composure and precision as if they had been quietly seated in their cabinets at Paris. Their observations on the force of terrestrial magnetism show most satisfactorily its deep source and wide extensions. The identity of the constitution of the atmosphere to a vast altitude was likewise ascertained. The facts noted by Gay-Lussac, relative to the state of the thermometer at different heights, appear generally to confirm the law which theory assigns for the gradation of temperature in the atmosphere: but many interesting points were left untouched by this philosopher. We are sorry that he had not carried with him the *cyanometer*, which enabled Saussure to determine the colour of the sky on the summits of the Swiss mountains. Still more we regret that he was not provided with an hygrometer and a photometer, of Leslie's construction. These delicate instruments could not have failed, in his hands, to furnish important data for discovering the relative dryness and transparency of the different strata of air. It would have been extremely interesting, at such a tremendous height, to have measured with accuracy the feeble light reflected from the azure canopy of heaven, and the intense force of the sun's direct rays, and hence to have determined what portion of them is

Montgolfier's Faubourg St. Antoine balloon (top) AERO-STATION, *third edition* (1788–97).

absorbed in their passage through the lower and denser atmosphere.

AERONAUTICS, supplement to fourth, fifth and sixth editions (1816–24). By Sir John Leslie (1766–1822), professor of natural philosophy at Edinburgh university and corresponding member of the Royal Institute of France, notable for his research on the radiation of heat. [For a concise history of balloon flights *see* the article BALLOON in the 1963 printing of *Encyclopaedia Britannica*.]

Boarding a Ship

Boarding a *ship*, is entering an enemy's ship in a fight. In boarding, it is best to bear up directly with him, and to cause all your ports to leeward to be beat open; then bring as many guns from your weather side as you have ports for; and laying the enemy's ship, on board, loof for loof, order your tops and yards to be manned and furnished with necessaries; and let all your small shot be in a readiness; then charge at once with both small and great, and at the same time enter your men under cover of the smoke, either on the bow of your enemy's ship, or bring your midship close up with her quarter, and so enter your men by the shrouds: or if you would use your ordnance, it is best to board your enemy's ship athwart her hawse; for in

that case you may use most of your great guns, and she only those of her prow. Let some of your men endeavour to cut down the enemy's yards and tackle, whilst others clear the decks, and beat the enemy from aloft. Then let the scuttles and hatches be broke open with all possible speed to avoid trains, and the danger of being blown up by barrels of powder placed under the decks.

BOARDING, first edition (1768–71).

The Midshipman in Nelson's Time

On his first entrance in a ship of war, every midshipman has several disadvantageous circumstances to encounter. These are partly occasioned by the nature of the sea-service; and partly by the mistaken prejudices of people in general respecting naval discipline, and the genius of sailors and their officers. No character, in their opinion, is more excellent than that of the common sailor, whom they generally suppose to be treated with great severity by his officers, drawing a comparison between them not very advantageous to the latter. The midshipman usually comes aboard tinctured with these prejudices, especially if his education has been amongst the higher rank of people; and if the officers happen to answer his opinion, he conceives an early disgust to the service, from a very partial and incompetent view of its operations. Blinded by these prepossessions, he is thrown off his guard, and very soon surprised to find, amongst those honest sailors, a crew of abandoned miscreants, ripe for any mischief or villainy. Perhaps, after a little observation, many of them will appear to him equally destitute of gratitude, shame or justice, and only deterred from the commission of any crime by the terror of severe punishment. He will discover, that the pernicious example of a few of the vilest in a ship of war is too often apt to poison the principles of the greatest number, especially if the reins of discipline are too much relaxed, so as to foster that idleness and dissipation, which engender sloth, diseases, and an utter profligacy of manners. If the midshipman on many occasions is obliged to mix with these, particularly in the exercises of extending or reducing the sails in the tops, he ought resolutely to guard against this contagion, with which the morals of his inferiors may be infected. He should, however, avail himself of their knowledge, and acquire their expertness in managing and fixing the sails and rigging, and never suffer himself to be excelled by an inferior. He will probably find a virtue in almost every private sailor, which is entirely unknown to many of his officers: that virtue is emulation, which is not indeed mentioned amongst their qualities by the gentlemen of *terra firma*, by whom their characters are often copiously described with very little judgment. There is hardly a common tar who is not envious of superior skill in his fellows, and jealous on all occasions to be outdone in what he considers as a branch of his duty: nor is he more afraid of the dreadful consequences of whistling in a storm, than of being stigmatised with the opprobrious epithet of *lubber*. Fortified against this scandal, by a thorough knowledge of his business, the sailor will sometimes sneer in private at the execution of orders which to him appear aukward, improper, or unlike a seaman. Nay, he will perhaps be malicious enough to suppress his own judgment, and, by a punctual obedience to command, execute whatever is to be performed in a manner which he knows to be improper, in order to expose the person commanding to disgrace and ridicule. Little skilled in the method of the schools, he considers the officer who cons his lesson by rote as very ill qualified for his station, because particular situations might render it necessary for the said officer to assist in putting his own orders in practice. An ignorance in this practical knowledge will therefore necessarily be thought an unpardonable deficiency by those who are to follow his directions. Hence the midshipman who associates with these sailors in the tops will be often entertained with a number of scurrilous jests, at the expence of his superiors. Hence also he will learn, that a timely application to those exercises can only prevent him from appearing in the same despicable point of view, which must certainly be a cruel mortification to a man of the smallest sensibility.

MIDSHIPMAN, second edition (1777–83).

Diving

Fig. 1. shows Dr. Haley's diving bell, with the divers at work. D B L K M P represents the body of the bell. D, the glass which serves as a window.

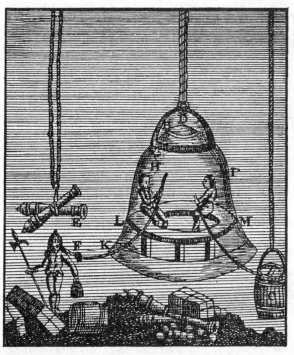

Fig. 1. Dr. Haley's diving bell. Fig. 2. Mr. Spalding's diving bell, an improvement on Dr. Haley's, at work. From DIVING, *second edition* (1777–83).

B, the cock for letting out the air which has been breathed. LM, the seats. C, one of the two air-barrels lowered alternately to supply air. P, H, two of the divers. F, another diver at a distance from the bell, and breathing through the flexible tube K. This diver is supposed to have a head-piece of lead, made to fit quite close about his shoulders: this head-piece was capable of containing as much air as would supply him for a minute or two: When he had occasion for more air he turned a cock at F, by which means a communication was opened with the air in the bell, and thus, he could receive a new supply at pleasure.

DIVING, second edition (1777–83).

One of the best of these contrivances is perhaps that proposed by M. Klingert, and described in a pamphlet published at Breslau in 1798 . . . The chief peculiarity in this machine is the mode in which fresh air is supplied, and respiration effected. This is done by two distinct flexible pipes proceeding from the inside of the helmet to the surface of the water; the one is for inhaling the air, and terminates in an ivory mouthpiece, which the diver may embrace with his lips and inhale the air; the other enters the helmet at the same place, and opens merely into the inside of the machine, so as to allow the foul air to be discharged. The diver, therefore, draws in the fresh air by the mouth, and discharges it into the helmet by the nostrils; and from the interior of the machine it is propelled by the act of inspiration, the expansion of the chest contracting the space between it and the armour, and forcing out exactly as much air as is drawn in, keeping up always a due equilibrium.

DIVING, seventh edition (1830–42).

Steam Navigation

Men of science, however, endeavoured to demonstrate that the navigation of the Atlantic by steam-power alone, was the dream of a visionary, and the tide of public opinion seemed to set in in the same belief; but a strong undercurrent was at work, and in 1838 the following advertisement appeared in the daily papers: "*Steam to New York.* the well-known steam-ship, *Sirius,* Lieutenant Roberts, R.N., Commander, is intended to leave London for New York on Wednesday 28th March, calling at Cork harbour, and to start from thence on Monday the 2nd of April, returning from New York the 1st of May." The *Sirius* was not expressly built for transatlantic navigation; she

Klingert's apparatus. From DIVING, *seventh edition* (1830–42).

belonged to the St. George Steam-Packet Company, and had run with a good reputation between London and Cork. Her tonnage was about 700 tons, and her engine about 320 horse power. Although advertised to sail on March 28th, circumstances delayed her departure till the morning of the 4th April, when she started at ten o'clock. Though first in the race, she was only three days in advance in starting; for on the 7th of the same month, the *Great Western,* built and fitted expressly for the purpose, followed her. In the interval, between the sailing of these vessels and the reports of their arrivals, much doubt prevailed as to the possibility of their accomplishing their task in safety, and the uncertainty was increased by vessels having arrived from America at ports in Britain, without having encountered either of the steamships; people having, for a moment, forgotten that there were more roads than one across the Atlantic. They were at length, however, spoken with by the *Westminster,* the *Sirius* on the 21st, within six hours' sail of New York, and the *Great Western* on the 22nd; and in due time, reports of their having reached New York arrived, the *Sirius* on the 22nd, being 17 days clear on the passage, and the *Great Western* on the 23rd, being 15 days.

STEAM NAVIGATION, seventh edition (1830–42).

Dating the Creation

Concerning the number of years which have elapsed since the creation of the world, there have been many disputes. The compilers of the Universal History determine it to have taken place in the year 4305 B.C. so that, according to them, the world is now in the 6096th year of its age. Others think it was created only 4000 years B.C. so that it hath not yet attained its 6000th year. Be this as it will, however, the whole account of the creation rests on the truth of the Mosaic history; and which we must of necessity accept, because we can find no other which does not either abound with the grossest absurdities, or lead us into absolute darkness. The Chinese and Egyptian pretensions to antiquity are so absurd and ridiculous, that the bare reading must be a sufficient confutation of them to every reasonable person. Some historians and philosophers are inclined to discredit the Mosaic accounts, from the appearances of volcanoes, and other natural phaenomena: but their objections are by no means sufficient to invalidate the authority of the sacred writings; not to mention that every one of their own systems is liable to insuperable objections. It is therefore reasonable for every person to accept of the Mosaic account of the creation as truth: but an historian is under an absolute necessity of doing it, because, without it, he is quite destitute of any standard or scale by which he might reduce the chronology of different nations to any agreement; and, in short, without receiving this account as true, it would be in a manner impossible at this day to write a general history of the world.

HISTORY, second edition (1777-83).

Longevity, with Some Outstanding Examples

From the different longevities of men in the beginning of the world, after the flood, and in these ages, Mr. Derham draws an argument for the interposition of a divine Providence.

Immediately after the creation, when the world was to be peopled by one man and one woman, the ordinary age was 900 and upwards.—Immediately after the flood, when there were three persons to stock the world, their age was cut shorter, and none of those patriarchs but Shem arrived at 500. In the second century we find none that reached 240: in the third, none but Terah that came to 200 years; the world, at least a part of it, by that time being so well peopled, that they had built cities, and were cantoned out into distant nations.—By degrees, as the number of people increased, their *longevity* dwindled, till it came down at length to 70 or 80 years: and there it stood and has continued to stand ever since the time of Moses.—This is found a good medium, and by means hereof the world is neither overstocked, nor kept too thin; but life and death keep a pretty equal pace.

LONGEVITY, third edition (1788-97).

Sedan Chair

Sedan chair, a vehicle supported by poles, wherein persons are carried; borne by two men. There are two hundred chairs allowed by act of parliament; and no

Names of the persons	Ages	Places of Abode	Living or Dead
Thomas Parr	152	Shropshire	Died November 14. 1635 Phil. Trans. No. 44.
Henry Jenkins	169	Yorkshire	Died December 8. 1670 Phil. Trans. No. 221.
Robert Montgomery	126	Ditto	Died in — — 1670
James Sands	140	Staffordshire	Do Fuller's Worthies
His Wife	120	Ditto	p. 47
Countess of Desmond	140	Ireland	Raleigh's Hist. p. 166
Ecleston	143	Ditto	Died — — 1691.
J. Sagar	112	Lancashire	— — — 1668.
— Laurence	140	Scotland	Living —
Simon Sack	141	Trionia	Died May 30. 1764
Col. Thomas Winslow	146	Ireland	— Aug. 26, 1766
Francis Consist	150	Yorkshire	— Jan. — 1768
Christ. J. Drakenberg	146	Norway	— June 24. 1660.
Margaret Forster	136	Cumberland	Both living 1771.
— her daughter	104	Ditto.	
Francis Bons	121	France	Died Feb. 6. 1769
John Brookey	134	Devonshire	Living — — 1777
James Bowels	152	Killingworth	Died Aug. 15. 1656
John Tice	125	Worcestershire	— March, 1774
John Mount	136	Scotland	— Feb. 27, 1776
A. Goldsmith	140	France	— June — 1776
Mary Yates	128	Shropshire	— — — 1776
John Bales	126	Northampton	— April 5, 1766
William Ellis	130	Liverpool	— Aug. 16, 1780
Louisa Truxo, a Negress	175	Tucomea, S. America	Living Oct. 5. 1780
Margaret Patten	138	Lockneugh near Paisley	Lynche's Guide to Health
Janet Taylor	108	Fintray, Scotland	Died Oct. 10, 1780
Richard Lloyd	133	Montgomery	Lynche's Guide to Health
Susannah Hilliar	100	Piddington, Northampsh.	Died Feb. 19. 1781
Ann Cockbolt	105	Stoke-Bruerne, *Ib.*	— April 5. 1775
James Hayley	112	Middlewich, Cheshire	— March 17. 1781

William Walker aged 112, not mentioned above, who was a soldier at the battle of Edge-hill

person is obliged to pay for a hackney-chair more than the rate allowed by the act for a hackney-coach driven two third parts of the said distance. . . . Their number is since increased, by 10 Ann. c. 19. and 12 Geo. 1. c. 12. to four hundred.

CHAIR, third edition (1788–97).

Hackney Coaches

Hackney coaches first began to ply in the streets of London, or rather waited at inns, in the year 1625, and were only 20 in number; but in 1635 they were so much increased, that king Charles issued out an order of council for restraining them. In 1637, he allowed 50 hackney-coachmen, each of whom might keep 12 horses. In 1652, their number was limited to 200; and in 1654, it was extended to 300. In 1661, 400 were licensed, at £5 annually for each. In 1694, 700 were allowed, and taxed by the 5 and 6 of W. & M. at £4 *per annum* each. By 9 Anne cap. 23. 800 coaches were allowed in London and Westminster; but by 8 Geo. III cap. 24. the number is increased to 1000, which are to be licensed by commissioners, and to pay a duty of 5s. per week to the king. On Sundays there were formerly only 175 hackney-coaches to ply, which were to be appointed by commissioners; but their number is now unlimited.

The fare of hackney coachmen in London, or within ten miles of the city, is 12 shillings and sixpence per day, allowing 12 hours per day. By the hour it is 1s. 6d. for the first, and 1s. for every hour after; and none are obliged to pay above 1s. for any distance not exceeding a mile and a half; or above 1s. 6d. for any distance not exceeding two miles. Where hackney coachmen refuse to go at, or exact more than their limited hire, they are subject to a forfeit not under 10s. nor exceeding £3 and which the commissioners have power to determine. Every hackney-coach must be provided with check strings [a cord from the coachman's sleeve to the passenger] and every coachman plying without them incurs a penalty of 5s. Drivers of hackney-coaches are to give way to persons of quality and gentlemen's coaches, under the penalty of £5.

The duty arising from licences to hackney-coaches and chairs in London, forms a branch of the king's extraordinary and perpetual revenue. This revenue is governed by commissioners of its own, and is in truth a benefit to the subject; as the expence of it is felt by no individual, and its necessary regulations have established a competent jurisdiction, whereby a very refractory race of men may be kept in some tolerable order.

HACKNEY, second edition (1777–83).

Coaches

Coaches have had the fate of all other inventions, to be brought by degrees to their perfection; at present they seem to want nothing, either with regard to ease or magnificence.

COACH, second edition (1777–83).

Early Railways

A railway is a species of road or carriage-way, in which the track of the carriage-wheels being laid with bars, or rails, of wood, stone, or metal, the carriage is more easily drawn along this smooth surface than over an ordinary road. . . .

The railways in Britain are so numerous, that it would exceed our limits to specify the particular lines. In the Newcastle coal district, on the river Wear, in the coal and mining districts of Yorkshire and Lancashire, as well as of Derbyshire and Staffordshire, there are numerous railways branching off from the navigable rivers and canals to the different mines. . . .

On some of the railways near Newcastle, the waggons are drawn by means of a steam-engine working in a waggon by itself, the wheels of which are driven by the engine, and acting on a rack laid along the railway, impel forward both the engine and the attached waggons: in some cases the wheels of the waggon operate without rail work, by the mere friction between them and the railway. The steam-engines employed for this purpose are of the high pressure kind; these requiring no condensing apparatus. But this application of steam has not yet arrived at such perfection as to have brought it into general use.

RAILWAY, supplement to the fourth, fifth and sixth editions (1816–24). By George Buchanan (1790?–1852), distinguished civil engineer and fellow of the Royal Society of Edinburgh.

First Modern Railways

In treating of the construction and mode of working railways, we shall confine ourselves principally to those which are intended for the transit of passengers and goods, and which are now [c.1840] opening so vast a field for the improvement of the human race; an improvement, in fact, entering into all the relations between man and man, and which no one, be he ever so sanguine, can venture to fix a limit to.

Possessing little general interest, and chiefly benefiting individuals, the attention railways attracted was principally confined to the parties immediately connected with them. But how different is the prospect now before us, since we have seen the magnificent creations of George Stephenson? Pack-horses are still the only mode of transit for traffic in many parts of the world; and within seventy years this was the general mode of conveyance for the carrying trade to Yorkshire and Lancashire from the west of England and Birmingham. In the year 1830, when the London and Birmingham railway was projected, the expense of constructing it was stated at £6,000 per mile with one line of rails, which were to be worked by horses, and warranted to go eight miles an hour; now the public are complaining of going *only* twenty miles an hour, and we have a right to expect that, at no very distant period, this velocity will at least be doubled; in fact, at the rate improvements have been advancing for the last few years, we know not where to place a limit of increase in speed.

When a railway is proposed between any two places, the public want to know how to distinguish between a bubble speculation, got up by a few interested individuals, a crudely-formed and hastily-adopted, but really good project, and a line got up with care and attention through all its parts, shewing it to be the result of patient research and of matured judgment; and according as inquirers find the following directions more or less attended to, they may place confidence in the scheme which is laid before them. . . .

There are many very great hardships connected with obtaining an act of incorporation for a railway. Parliament requires that a plan and section of every part of the ground through which the intended line is to pass, shall be lodged with their clerk, and with the clerks of the peace in every county through which the railway goes. This is a very proper regulation, in order that every landholder may be able, by travelling a convenient distance, to have a personal inspection of a duly authorised document, so as to examine the nature and extent of the benefit, or the inconvenience which it may occasion to his particular property; but parliament should at the same time have given the railway companies the power of complying with this wholesome regulation, in the same way as road surveys are made in Ireland, by an order from two magistrates to enter any requisite grounds. This, however, is not done, and therefore it follows, as a necessary consequence, that the projectors of these undertakings, no matter how beneficial or important soever to the community at large, are left entirely at the mercy of the landholders, whether they can make their survey or not. We have ourselves known, that when decided opposition has been evinced to the undertaking, the engineers and surveyors have been put to all possible shifts to obtain the necessary data for their plans and sections. Working by night with lanthorns has even been unavoidably resorted to; and in one case, where the proprietor was a clergyman, he was watched on Sunday until he went into his church, and a strong party immediately setting to work, just succeeded in finishing the business as he concluded his sermon.

The facilities of opposing a bill in parliament are so great, that every temptation is held out to do so, especially when the rich harvest to counsel, solicitors, and witnesses, is considered; and as has been well observed by the Irish railway commissioners, discussions are mooted of the most discursive and discordant kinds, relating to all the abstract professional matter in the most distant manner connected with a railway. The principles of curves and gradients are entered into with mathematical precision, and the laws

A locomotive engine, from RAILWAY, *seventh edition* (1830–42).

of friction and gravity are investigated; questions about which the counsel and the court are often equally ignorant, the one side seeking to swell the estimates and lower the profits, and the other pulling in the opposite direction, like the bulls and bears on the stock exchange, till at last, probably after the expenditure of thousands, the bill is thrown out, not on its own merits or demerits, but because, perhaps, a notice to the proprietor of five or six yards of a cabbage garden, was left next door by mistake.

The parliamentary rules are now as much too strict, as they were at first too loose. The time when the required plans and sections are to be deposited, is very inconvenient; two years at least being required between the deposits being paid and the act obtained. Thus, at the present time, if any line is wished to be procured, the surveys must be made in the autumn of 1838, the plans must be lodged and the notices given in March 1839, the petition for the bill presented to the Commons in February 1840, and supposing the act obtained the same session, little if any real work can be done until the spring of 1841. . . .

When the intended line is once decided on, the surveyors should be sent out as speedily as possible; and these are followed by the levellers, who are the engineers. It will be best to survey wide, when you are not quite certain of the exact position of the line; the surveyors give in their plans to the engineers, who proceed to lay down upon them the line as their levelling goes on, taking care as nearly as possible to balance the cuttings and embankments. It will save the engineers a deal of trouble, if, where curves are to be run, a man is sent a-head to put in marks at short distances, giving him the measure from the nearest hedge on the plan, which measure he takes on the ground, and sticks in his mark.

The survey, with complete plans and book of reference, containing the land for at least three times the width required for the railway, shewing every field numbered for each parish, with its owner and occupier, ought not to cost more than £15 per mile. The best plan will be to survey as wide as is intended to apply for a power of deviation in the act of parliament.

RAILWAYS, seventh edition (1830–42). By Peter Lecount.

The Railway Engine-man

The engine-man should always stand by his hand-gear whilst the engine is running, and keep a most vigilant look out before him, passing all out-stations or stopping places slowly, and upon discovering any train at a stand still, he should approach and pass it at no greater speed than three miles an hour. Should any train require the assistance of a ballast-engine, it should be immediately given on an application to that effect from the upper guard, the engine-man first placing his waggons on a siding; but the ballast-engine should not draw the train any farther than is necessary to place it under the charge of a regular passenger or

goods' engine; and it should then return to its waggons in such a manner as not to interfere with the next train coming along the line. During a fog the engine should be moved slowly, and the whistle be blown at not greater intervals than a quarter of a mile. Fogs, however, will always be dangerous on railways till two whistles totally different in sound are used, one for each line, blowing by machinery at every eighth part of a mile. When the ballast-engines stop in a fog on the line, the fireman should be sent at least 400 yards a-head to look out.

It is the duty of the engine-man to take care that the engines are in a proper state of cleanliness and efficiency before they quit the engine-house, that every part is in proper and complete working order, and that the regular supply of coke and water is in both the engine and the tender, together with the requisite quantity of oil and waste; and he should personally inspect his tool-box, and ascertain that every thing is in it which by right should be so, and that his shovels, rakes, &c. are in readiness. According to the distance the engine-house is from the point where he hooks on the train, time must be allowed him before the minute of departure sufficient to let him arrive at the required spot about one minute before he is wanted, and no more.

He should be very careful in bringing his engine down to the head of the train, where the connection should be made by a man specially appointed for the purpose. He should leave his condensed steam cock open as long as he can, being very cautious that it is shut just before the time of departure. During the journey he, in conjunction with his fireman, should keep a vigilant look-out for all signals of danger, watching each policeman as he approaches him till he has made his notification that all is in security along his part of the line. He must be attentive to stopping the train at the places ordered, and that he does not exceed the regulated speed, considering correctness of arrival his greatest aim, and consequently making up as far as he can in one part of his journey for any unavoidable detentions which may have arisen in other parts.

He should be constantly alert to the signals from the guard of the train, and ready to stop it in the shortest possible time when ordered to do so. The guard should have a check-string to the arm of the engine-man, and a flexible hollow tube should be fixed from the guard's carriage to the engine, through which the men can converse, which the noise of the engine and train will otherwise render difficult.

RAILWAYS, seventh edition (1830–42). By Peter Lecount.

Process of Making Alum

At Whitby, in Yorkshire, alum is made thus: Having burnt a quantity of the ore with whins, or wood, till it becomes white, then they barrow it in a pit, where it is steeped in water for eight or ten hours.

This liquor, or lixivium, is conveyed by troughs to the alum-house, into cisterns, and from them into the pans, where it is boiled about 24 hours. They add a certain quantity of the lee of kelp; the whole is drawn off into a settler; where having remained about an hour, that the sulphur and other dregs may have time to settle to the bottom, it is conveyed into coolers. This done, to every tun of the liquor they add about eight gallons of urine; and having stood four days and nights, till quite cool, the alum begins to crystallize on the sides of the vessel, from which being scraped off, it is washed with fair water, and then thrown in a bing, to let the water drain off. After this it is thrown into a pan, called the roching pan, and there melted; in which state it is conveyed by troughs into tuns, where it stands about 10 days, till perfectly condensed. Then staving the tuns, the alum is taken out, chipped, and carried to the store-houses.

This is what we commonly call roche or rock alum, as being prepared from stones cut from the rocks of the quarry; and stands contradistinguished from the common alum, or that prepared from earths.

ALUM, first edition (1768–71).

Process of Making Armoniac

The modern sal armoniac is entirely factitious, and made in Egypt; where several long-necked glass bottles, being filled with soot, a little sea-salt, and the urine of cattle, and having their mouth luted with a piece of wet cotton, are placed over an oven or furnace, contrived for the purpose, in a thick bed of ashes, nothing but the necks appearing, and kept there two days and a night, with a continual strong fire. The steam swells up the cotton, and forms a paste at the vent-hole, hindering the salts from evaporating; which, being confined, stick to the top of the bottle, and are, upon breaking it, taken out in those large cakes, which they send to England. Only soot exhaled from dung, is the proper ingredient in this preparation; and the dung of camels affords the strongest and best.

ARMONIAC, first edition (1768–71).

Bird-Lime

Bird-lime, a viscid substance, prepared after different ways. The most common bird-lime among us, is made from holly-bark, boiled ten or twelve hours; when the green coat being separated from the other, it is covered up a fortnight in a moist place, then pounded into a tough paste, so that no fibres of the wood are discernible, and washed in a running stream till no motes appear; put up to ferment four or five days, skimmed as often as any thing arises, and laid up for use. To use it, a third part of nut-oil, or thin grease, must be incorporated with it over the fire.

BIRD-LIME, first edition (1768–71).

Bird-Catching in 1800

In the suburbs of London (and particularly about Shoreditch) are several weavers and other tradesmen, who, during the months of October and March, get their livelihood by an ingenious, and, we may say, a scientific, method of *bird-catching*, which is totally unknown in other parts of Great Britain. The reason of this trade being confined to so small a compass, arises from there being no considerable sale of singing-birds except in the metropolis: as the apparatus for this purpose is also heavy, and at the same time must be carried on a man's back, it prevents the bird-catchers going to above three or four miles distance.

The nets are a most ingenious piece of mechanism; are generally twelve yards and a half long, and two yards and a half wide; and no one, on bare inspection, would imagine that a bird (who is so very quick in all its motions) could be catched by the nets flapping over each other, till he becomes eye-witness of the pullers seldom failing.

The wild birds *fly* (as the bird-catchers term it) chiefly during the month of October, and part of September and November; as the flight in March is much less considerable than that of Michaelmas. It is to be noted also, that the several species of birds of *flight* do not make their appearance precisely at the same time, during the months of September, October, and November. The pippet, for example, begins to fly about Michaelmas; and then the woodlark, linnet, goldfinch, chaffinch, greenfinch, and other birds of flight succeed; all of which are not easily to be caught, or in any numbers, at any other time, and more particularly the pippet and the woodlark. [The phenomenon of migration was evidently not properly understood.]

The bird-catcher, who is a substantial man, and hath a proper apparatus for this purpose, generally carries with him five or six linnets, (of which more are caught than any singing bird), two gold-finches, two green-finches, one wood-lark, one red-poll, a yellow-hammer, tit-lark, and aberdavine, and perhaps a bull-finch; these are placed at small distances from the nets in little cages. He hath, besides, what are called *flur-birds*, which are placed within the nets, are raised upon the flur, and gently let down at the time the wild bird approaches them. These generally consist of the linnet, the gold-finch, and the green-finch, which are secured to the flur by what is called a *brace*; a contrivance that secures the birds without doing any injury to their plumage.

It having been found that there is a superiority between bird and bird, from the one being more in song than the other; the bird-catchers contrive that their call-birds should moult before the usual time. They therefore, in June or July, put them into a close box under two or three folds of blankets, and leave their dung in the cage to raise a greater heat; in which state they continue, being perhaps examined but once a-week to have fresh water. As for food, the air is so putrid, that they eat little during the whole state of

Bird-catching in the Faeroe Islands, from the third edition (1788–97).

confinement, which lasts about a month. The birds frequently die under the operation; and hence the value of a stopped bird rises greatly. When the bird hath thus prematurely moulted, he is in song whilst the wild birds are out of song, and his note is louder and more piercing than that of a wild one; but it is not only in his note he receives an alteration, the plumage is equally improved. The black and yellow in the wings of the gold-finch, for example, become deeper and more vivid, together with a most beautiful gloss, which is not to be seen in the wild bird. The bill, which in the latter is likewise black at the end, in the stopped-bird becomes white and more taper, as do its legs: in short, there is as much difference between a wild and a stopped-bird, as there is between a horse which is kept in body-clothes and one at grass.

When the bird-catcher hath laid his nets, he disposes of his call-birds at proper intervals. It must be owned that there is most malicious joy in these call-birds to bring the wild ones into the same state of captivity; . . .

Their sight and hearing infinitely excel that of the bird-catcher. The instant that the wild birds are perceived, notice is given by one to the rest of the call-birds, (as it is by the first hound that hits on the scent to the rest of the pack); after which, follows the same

sort of tumultuous ecstacy and joy. The call-birds, while the bird is at a distance, do not sing as a bird does in a chamber; they invite the wild ones by what the bird-catchers call *short jerks*, which, when the birds are good, may be heard at a great distance. The ascendency by this call or invitation is so great, that the wild bird is stopped in its course of flight; and, if not already acquainted with the nets, lights boldly within 20 yards of perhaps three or four bird-catchers, on a spot which otherwise it would not have taken the least notice of. Nay, it frequently happens, that if half a flock only are caught, the remaining half will immediately afterwards light in the nets, and share the same fate; and should only one bird escape, that bird will suffer itself to be pulled at till it is caught; such a fascinating power have the call-birds. . . .

The manner of bird-catching in the Faroe islands is so very strange and hazardous, that the description should by no means be omitted. Necessity compels mankind to wonderful attempts. The cliffs which contain the objects of their search are often two hundred fathoms in height, and are attempted from above and below. In the first case, the fowlers provide themselves with a rope 80 or 100 fathoms in length. The fowler fastens one end about his waist and between his legs, recommends himself to the protection of the Almighty, and is lowered down by six others, who place a piece of timber on the margin of the rock, to preserve the rope from wearing against the sharp edge. They have besides a small line fastened to the body of the adventurer, by which he gives signals that they may lower or raise him, or shift him from place to place. The last operation is attended with great danger, by the loosening of the stones, which often fall on his head, and would infallibly destroy him, was it not protected by a strong thick cap; but even that is found unequal to save him against the weight of the larger fragments of rock. The dexterity of the fowlers is amazing; they will place their feet against the front of the precipice, and dart themselves some fathoms from it, with a cool eye survey the places where the birds nestle, and again shoot into their haunts. In some places the birds lodge in deep recesses. The fowler will alight there, disengage himself from the rope, fix it to a stone, and at his leisure collect the booty, fasten it to his girdle, and resume his pendulous seat. At times he will again spring from the rock, and in that attitude, with a fowling-net placed at the end of a staff, catch the old birds which are flying to and from their retreats. When he hath finished his dreadful employ, he gives a signal to his friends above, who pull him up, and share the hard-earned profit. The feathers are preserved for exportation: the flesh is partly eaten fresh, but the greater portion dried for winter's provision.

BIRD, third edition (1788–97).

On Hunting

Nature has prepared many advantages and pleasures for the use of mankind, and given them the taste to enjoy them, and the sagacity to improve them; but of all the out-of-door amusements that have occupied the modern world, at least the male part of it, nothing has better stood the test of time than the noble diversion of hunting.

"Of all our fond diversions,
A hunter's is the best;
In spite of wars and petty jars,
That sport has stood the test."

And why has it stood the test? Not merely because the passion for the chase is interwoven closely with our nature; not because it originated in necessity, therefore originated in nature; but because it has been encouraged and approved of by the very best authorities, and practised by the greatest men. It cannot now, then, be supposed to dread criticism, or require support; neither can any solid objections be raised against a reasonable enjoyment of the sports of the field in general, provided what ought to be the pleasing relaxation of a man's leisure hours be not converted into the whole business of his life. But hunting, above all others, is a taste characteristically manly and appropriate to the gentlemen of Great Britain; and it has likewise another advantage over all other sports of the

field, which adds much to its value in this land of liberty, and especially in the present age: it is a kind of Saturnalian amusement, in which the privileges of rank and fortune are laid aside, the best man in the chase being he who rides the best horse, and is best skilled in the use he should make of his superiority.

HUNTING, seventh edition (1830–42). By Charles Apperley (1777–1843), the once-famed "Nimrod", writer on the chase and on the turf.

Remains of Giants

January 11. 1613, some masons digging near the ruins of a castle in Dauphiné, France, in a field which (by tradition) had long been called *the giant's field*, at the depth of 18 feet discovered a brick-tomb 30 feet long, 12 feet wide, and 8 feet high; on which was a grey stone, with the words *Theutobochus Rex* cut thereon. When the tomb was opened, they found a human skeleton entire, 25 feet and a half long, 10 feet wide across the shoulders, and five feet deep from the breast-bone to the back. His teeth were about the size each of an ox's foot, and his shin bone measured four feet.—Near Mazarino, in Sicily, in 1516, was found a giant 30 feet high; his head was the size of an hoghead, and each of his teeth weighed five ounces. Near Palermo, in the valley of Mazara, in Sicily, a skeleton of a giant 30 feet long was found, in the year 1548; and another of 33 feet high, in 1550; and many curious persons have preserved several of these gigantic bones.

The Athenians found near their city two famous skeletons, one of 34 and the other of 36 feet high.

At Totu, in Bohemia, in 758, was found a skeleton, the head of which could scarce be encompassed by the arms of two men together, and whose legs, which they still keep in the castle of that city, were 26 feet long. The skull of the giant found in Macedonia, September 1691, held 210 pounds of corn.

The celebrated Sir Hans Sloane, who treated this matter very learnedly, does not doubt these facts; but thinks the bones were those of elephants, whales, or other enormous animals.

Elephants' bones may be shown for those of giants; but they can never impose on connoisseurs. Whales, which, by their immense bulk, are more proper to be substituted for the largest giants, have neither arms nor legs, and the head of that animal hath not the least resemblance to that of a man. If it be true, therefore, that a great number of the gigantic bones which we have mentioned have been seen by anatomists, and by them have been reputed real human bones, the existence of giants is proved.

GIANT, second edition (1777–83).

Character of Rabelais

It is the peculiar misfortune of distinguished humourists to have the paternity of such jests as are tossing unclaimed about the world laid to their charge.

They become a sort of Foundling Hospitals for Wit; and Rabelais has had more than his share of this abandoned progeny thrust upon him. His reputation as a man has suffered accordingly, and this for an obvious reason; for just in the degree that a great man's mind is marked by features, which puzzle the finest sagacity to discriminate and reconcile, are people disposed to pronounce an authoritative judgment regarding him. In all such cases, a lively anecdote, or sparkling witticism, is too cheap and pleasant a method of settling a doubtful character, not to be generally adopted. One common character runs throughout all the anecdotes of which Rabelais is the hero. They show a mind without gravity or depth, giving head to its most wayward sallies, neglectful of self-respect, and reckless of present circumstances, or of possible results. Such is just the character which a superficial observer is likely to form of him from his own romance. The rhodomantade, the coarseness, the downright nonsense, the reckless exuberance of humour, are easily noted; whilst the vein of deep and earnest thought that ever and anon shows itself amid the surrounding extravagance, the infinite good sense, the high-toned and enlightened philanthropy, and the great moral purpose which the author had in view, escape the careless and unpenetrating eye. The vices, which he has laid bare with such masterly tact, have been set down as his own, and he is charged with having been a profligate, a debauchee, and a buffoon, destitute alike of self-respect, and reverence for whatsoever is sacred or noble. But every thing that is known of his life, as well as what may be inferred from a study of his works, goes to discountenance such a conclusion.

RABELAIS, seventh edition (1830–42). By Theodore Martin.

Bunyan's Pilgrim's Progress

Before he left his prison Bunyan had begun the book which has made his name immortal. The history of that book is remarkable. The author was, as he tells us, writing a treatise, in which he had occasion to speak of the stages of the Christian progress. He compared that progress, as many others had compared it, to a pilgrimage. Soon his quick wit discovered innumerable points of similarity which had escaped his predecessors. Images came crowding on his mind faster than he could put them into words, quagmires and pits, steep hills, dark and horrible glens, soft vales, sunny pastures, a gloomy castle of which the courtyard was strewn with the skulls and bones of murdered prisoners, a town all bustle and splendour, like London on the Lord Mayor's Day, and the narrow path, straight as a rule could make it, running on up hill and down hill, through city and through wilderness, to the Black River and the Shining Gate.

He had no assistance. Nobody but himself saw a line till the whole was complete. He then consulted his pious friends. Some were pleased. Others were much scandalized. It was a vain story, a mere romance, about giants, and lions, and goblins, and warriors, sometimes fighting with monsters, and sometimes regaled by fair ladies in stately palaces. The loose atheistical wits at Will's might write such stuff to divert the painted Jezebels of the court; but did it become a minister of the gospel to copy the evil fashions of the world? There had been a time when the cant of such fools would have made Bunyan miserable. But that time was passed; and his mind was now in a firm and healthy state. He saw that, in employing fiction to make truth clear and goodness attractive, he was only following the example which every Christian ought to propose to himself; and he determined to print.

The *Pilgrim's Progress* stole silently into the world. Not a single copy of the first edition [1678] is known to be in existence. It is probable that, during some months, the little volume circulated only among poor and obscure sectaries. But soon the irresistible charm of a book which gratified the imagination of the reader with all the action and scenery of a fairy tale, which exercised his ingenuity by setting him to discover a multitude of curious analogies, which interested his feelings for human beings, frail like himself, and struggling with temptations from within and from without, which every moment drew a smile from him by some stroke of quaint yet simple pleasantry, and nevertheless left on his mind a sentiment of reverence for God and of sympathy for man, began to produce its effect.

It is a significant circumstance that, till a recent period, all the numerous editions of the *Pilgrim's Progress* were evidently meant for the cottage and the servants' hall. The paper, the printing, the plates, were all of the meanest description. In general, when the educated minority and the common people differ about the merit of a book, the opinion of the educated minority finally prevails. The *Pilgrim's Progress* is perhaps the only book about which, after the lapse of a hundred years, the educated minority has come over to the opinion of the common people.

BUNYAN, JOHN, eighth edition (1853–60). By Lord Macaulay (1800–59), historian, essayist and politician.

The Instruction of Our First Parents

The earliest history of mankind, by far, that we possess, is that contained in the Book of Genesis. It is extremely brief and scanty; especially the earliest portion of it. But it plainly represents the first of the human race, when in the Garden of Eden, as receiving direct communications from God. We have no detailed account, however, of the instruction they received; and even part of what the history does record is but obscurely intimated. For example, it is rather hinted than expressly stated, that the use of language was imparted to them by revelation. This, however, is generally understood to be the meaning of the passage

(Gen. ii. 20), in which it is said that God brought unto Adam the beasts and birds, to see what he would call them, and that Adam gave them names.

But our first parents, or their children, must have received direct from God a great deal of instruction of which no particulars are related. For besides being taught something of religious and moral duty (Gen. ii. 16; iv. 7), it is evident that they must have learned something of the arts of life. The first generations of mankind were certainly not left at all in the condition of mere *savages*, subsisting on such wild fruits and animals as they might chance to meet with. We read concerning the first two sons of Adam, that the one was occupied in tilling the ground, and the other in keeping cattle.

And even independently of the Bible history, we might draw the same conclusion from what is matter of actual experience, and as it were before our eyes at this day. For it appears that mere savages, if left to themselves without any instruction, never did, and never can, civilise themselves. And, consequently, the *first* of the human race that did acquire any degree of civilisation, since they could not have had instruction from other *men*, must have had a super-human instructor. But for such an instructor, all mankind would have been savages at this day. The mere fact that civilised men do exist, is enough to prove, even to a person who had never heard of the Bible, that, at some time or other, men must have been taught something by a superior Being: in other words, that there must have been a *revelation*.

DISSERTATION; *exhibiting a general view of the Rise, Progress, and Corruptions of Christianity*, eighth edition (1853–60). By Richard Whately (1787–1863), logician and theological writer, and archbishop of Dublin.

Education

The end of education is to render the individual, as much as possible, an instrument of happiness, first to himself and next to other beings.

The properties, by which he is fitted to become an instrument to this end, are, partly, those of the body, and, partly, those of the mind.

Happiness depends upon the condition of the body, either immediately, as where the bodily powers are exerted for the attainment of some good; or mediately, through the mind, as where the condition of the body affects the qualities of the mind.

Education, in the sense in which it is usually taken, and in which it shall here be used, denotes the means which may be employed to render the *mind*, as far as possible, an operative cause of happiness.

Education, then . . . may be defined, the best employment of all the means which can be made use of, by man, for rendering the human mind to the greatest possible degree the cause of human happiness. Every thing, therefore, which operates, from the first germ of existence, to the final extinction of life, in such a manner as to affect those qualities of the mind on which happiness in any degree depends, comes within the scope of the present inquiry. The grand question of education embraces nothing less than this—namely, What can be done by the human powers, by aid of all the means which are at human disposal, to render the human mind the instrument of the greatest degree of happiness? It is evident, therefore, that nothing, of any kind, which operates at any period of life, however early, or however late, ought to be left out of the account. Happiness is too precious an effect, to let any cause of it, however small, run to waste and be lost. The means of human happiness are not so numerous

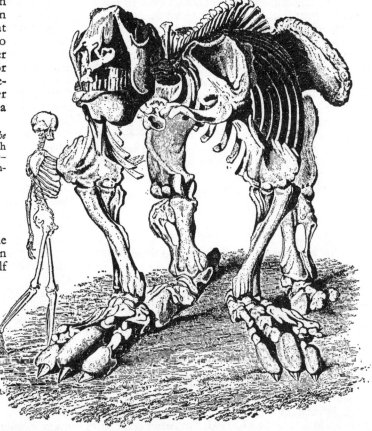

Megatherium, drawn from the specimen in the Royal Cabinet of Madrid. From ORGANIC REMAINS, FOSSIL, *supplement to the fourth, fifth and sixth editions* (1816–24).

that any of them can be spared. Not to turn every thing to account is here, if any where, bad economy, in the most emphatical sense of the phrase.

EDUCATION, supplement to the fourth, fifth and sixth editions (1816–24). By James Mill (1773–1836), historian, economist and philosopher, and father of John Stuart Mill.

School Teachers Underpaid

We will venture to say, that there is no class of men to whom a nation is so much indebted as to those employed in instructing the young: For if it be education that forms the only distinction between the civilized and the savage, much certainly is due to those who devote themselves to the office of instruction. It must be the duty therefore of every state to take care that proper encouragement be given to those who undertake this office. There ought to be such a salary as would render it an object of ambition to men of abilities and learning, or at least as would keep the teacher respectable. In Scotland, the office of a schoolmaster was formerly much more lucrative than at present, and most of that class had received liberal education; and this is the reason why the common people in Scotland have been famous even to a proverb, for their learning. But at present the salary of a country schoolmaster, independent of fees for scholars, is not greater than a ploughman can earn, being seldom more than £8 6s. 8d. the consequence of which is that this, which is in fact an honourable, because an useful profession, is now sinking into contempt. It is no longer an object to a man of learning; and we must soon be satisfied with schoolmasters that can read, write, and cast accounts, a little better than the lowest of the people, or who from some natural deformity are unable to exercise a trade. And what in this case must become of the minds of the common people? They must be totally uncultivated.

TEACHERS, fourth edition (1800–10).

Education of Ladies

Ladies have sometimes distinguished themselves as prodigies of learning. Many of the most eminent geniuses of the French nation have been of the female sex. Several of our countrywomen have also made a respectable figure in the republic of letters. Yet we cannot approve of giving girls a learned education. To acquire the accomplishments which are more proper for their sex, will afford sufficient employment for their earlier years. If they be instructed in the grammar of their mother-tongue, and taught to read and speak it with propriety; be taught to write a fair hand, and to perform with readiness the most useful operations of arithmetic: if they be instructed in the nature of the duties which they owe to God, to themselves, and to society; this will be almost all the literary instruction necessary for them. Yet we do not mean to forbid them an acquaintance with the literature of their

country. The periodical writers, who have taught all the duties of morality, the decencies of life, and the principles of taste, in so elegant and pleasing a manner, may with great propriety be put into the hands of our female pupil. Neither will we deny her the historians, the most popular voyages and travels, and such of our British poets as may be put into her hands without corrupting her heart or inflaming her passions. But could our opinion or advice have so much influence, we would endeavour to persuade our countrymen and countrywomen to banish from among them the novelists, those panders of vice, with no less determined severity than that with which Plato excludes the poets from his republic, or that with which the converts to Christianity, mentioned in the Acts, condemned their magical volumes to the flames. Unhappily, novels and plays are almost the only species of reading in which the young people of the present age take delight; and nothing has contributed more effectually to bring on that dissoluteness of manners which prevails among all ranks.

EDUCATION, third edition (1788–97).

Too Much Teaching of Latin

In regard to the mode of education in England, there is much both to commend and censure. Scotland has been for a century past in possession of a larger proportion of parish schools; but the utility of these is much lessened by an established routine of teaching Latin to almost all youths, whatever be their intended line of life. In England this absurdity is less prevalent, because most of the schools are private undertakings, the managers of which are necessarily guided by considerations of utility. The youth destined for a life of business are thus saved a serious waste of time; their education, if imperfect, is not supererogatory; but, on examining the higher seminaries of England, we find much ground for disappointment, and many marks of a blind adherence to ancient usage. Two universities are evidently inadequate to the education of the nobility, the gentry, and the clergy of so populous a country. Their course of study, also, is quite unsuitable to the future occupations of many of the students. They were originally designed for the education of churchmen; and, to this day, Latin and Greek, with the addition of mathematics at Cambridge, form the chief objects of instruction. In a country of which commerce forms the strength, there are no teachers of political economy. Under a government which has so long borne the representative form, there are no classses for the study of modern history, or the principles of legislation. There are here hardly any of those public lectures, which, in the rest of Europe, constitute the grand characteristic of a university, and distinguish it from schools:—all, or nearly all, is done by private tuition.

ENGLAND, supplement to the fourth, fifth and sixth editions (1816–24). By Joseph Lowe.

A Genealogical Table *of the different races of* Dogs

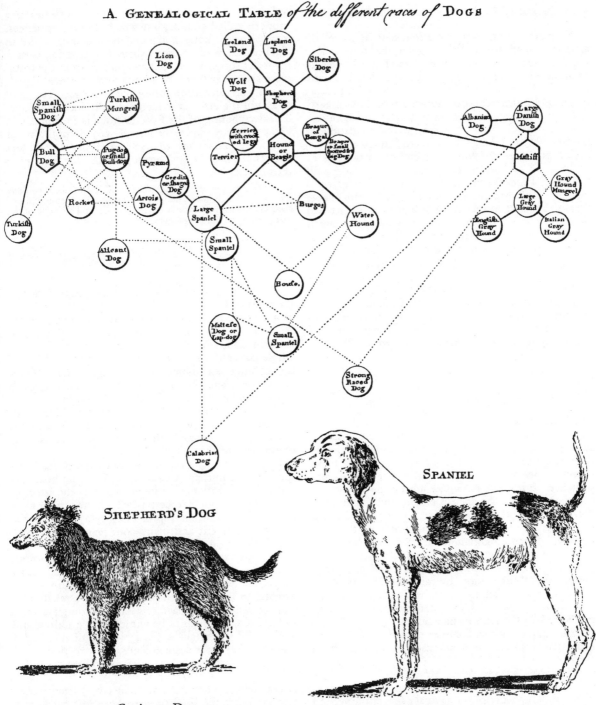

SHEPHERD'S DOG

SPANIEL

Canis, or Dog

Canis, or Dog, in zoology, a genus of quadrupeds, belonging to the order of ferae. The characters of the dog are these: He has six fore-teeth in the upper jaw, and those in the sides being longer than the intermediate ones, which are lobated; in the under jaw there are likewise six fore-teeth, those on the sides being lobated. He has six grinders in the upper, and seven in the lower jaw. The teeth called dog-teeth are four, one on each side, both in the lower and upper jaw; they are sharp-pointed, bent a little inward, and stand at a distance from any of the rest.

CANIS, first edition (1768–71).

Effects of Foreign Travel on the Young

Formerly young men were not sent to travel till after they had proceeded through the forms of a regular education, and had at least attained such an age that they were no longer to be considered as mere boys. But the progress of luxury, the desire of parents to introduce their children into the world at an early age that they may early attain to wealth and honours, and various other causes, have gradually introduced the practice of sending mere boys to foreign countries, under pretence of affording them opportunities of shaking off prejudices, of storing their minds with truly useful knowledge, and of acquiring those graceful manners and that manly address which will enable them to acquit themselves in a becoming manner when they are called to the duties of active life. How much travelling at such an early age contributes to fulfil the views of parents, a slight survey of the senate-house, the gambling-houses, the racecourse, and the cock-pit, will readily convince the sagacious observer.

But whose mind has been judiciously cultivated, and who has attained to maturity of judgement, if he set out on his travels with a view to obtain real improvements, and persist invariably in the prosecution of that view, cannot but derive very great advantage from travelling.

EDUCATION, third edition (1788–97).

Deciphering the Rosetta Stone

In the midst of all the zeal and activity displayed by our countrymen who have travelled, or who are resident, in Egypt, it is greatly to be deplored that their attention has not yet [c. 1816] been turned to an object, which is paramount to all the rest in its importance, for the substantial advancement of our acquaintance with the ancient history and literature of the country; that is, the recovery [1799] of the lost fragments or of some of the duplicates of the "trilinguar," or rather trigrammatic STONE OF ROSETTA; a monument which has already enabled us to obtain a general idea of the nature and subject of any given hieroglyphical inscription, by pursuing the investigations already carried to an unexpected extent by an anonymous author, whose interpretation was communicated to the Antiquarian Society by Mr. Rouse Boughton, together with copies of some fragments of manuscripts which this gentleman had brought from Egypt. (*Archaeologia*, Vol. XVIII. p. 61. *Museum Criticum*, No. VI and VII.) Mr De Sacy, and more especially Mr Akerblad, had made some progress in identifying the sense of the several parts of the second inscription of the stone; but they had scarcely at all considered the sacred characters, and it was left for British industry, to convert to permanent profit a monument, which had before been a useless, though a glorious trophy of British valour.

We must recollect that every analysis of an unknown object of this nature must unavoidably proceed more or less by the imperfect argumentation sometimes very properly called a circle, but which, in such instances, may be more aptly compared to a spiral, or to an algebraical approximation; since, by assuming certain incorrect suppositions, not too remote from the truth, we may render them, by means of a continual repetition of the calculation, more and more accurate, until at length the error is rendered wholly inconsiderable. The deciphering of the Rosetta stone is fortunately in great measure independent of any hypothesis of this kind extraneous to itself; and the Greek text affords at once the first approximation for beginning the process.

EGYPT, supplement to the fourth, fifth and sixth editions (1816–24). By Thomas Young (1773–1829), physicist and physician, known for his work in physical optics, and also one of the first partially to decipher Egyptian hieroglyphics.

How Pompey's Pillar at Alexandria was Climbed by British Sailors

But what most engages the attention of travellers is the pillar of Pompey, as it is commonly called, situated at a quarter of a league from the southern gate (of Alexandria). It is composed of red granite. The capital is Corinthian, with palm leaves, and not indented. The whole column is 114 feet high. One of the volutes of the column was immaturely brought down about twelve years ago [?1788], by a prank of some English captains, which is thus related by Mr. Irwin.

These jolly sons of Neptune had been pushing about the can on board one of the ships in the harbour, until a strange freak entered into one of their brains. The eccentricity of the thought occasioned it immediately to be adopted; and its apparent impossibility was but a spur for the putting it into execution. The boat was ordered; and with proper implements for the attempt, these enterprising heroes pushed ashore, to drink a bowl of punch on the top of Pompey's pillar! At the spot they arrived; and many contrivances were proposed to accomplish the desired point. But their labour was vain; and they began to despair of success, when the genius who struck out the frolic happily suggested the means of performing it. A man was dispatched to the city for a paper kite. The inhabitants were by this time apprized of what was going forward, and flocked in crowds to be witness of the address and boldness of the English. The governor of Alexandria was told that these seamen were about to pull down Pompey's pillar. But whether he gave them credit for their respect to the Roman warrior, or to the Turkish government, he left them to themselves; and politely answered that the English were too great patriots to injure the remains of Pompey. He knew little, however, of the disposition of the people who were engaged in this undertaking. Had the Turkish empire risen in opposition, it would not perhaps at that moment have deterred them. The kite was brought, and flown so directly over the pillar, that when it fell on the other side, the string lodged upon the capital.

The chief obstacle was now overcome. A two-inch rope was tied to one end of the string, and drawn over the pillar by the end to which the kite was affixed. By this rope one of the seamen ascended to the top; and in less than an hour a kind of shroud was constructed, by which the whole company went up, and drank their punch amid the shouts of the astonished multitude. To the eye below, the capital of the pillar does not appear capable of holding more than one man upon it; but our seamen found it could contain no less than eight persons very conveniently. It is astonishing that no accident befel these madcaps, in a situation so elevated, that would have turned a landman giddy in his sober senses. The only detriment which the pillar received, was the loss of the volute before mentioned; which came down with a thundering sound, and was carried to England by one of the captains, as a present to a lady who had commissioned him for a piece of the pillar. The discovery which they made amply compensated for this mischief; as without their evidence, the world would not have known at this hour, that there was originally a statue on this pillar, one foot and ancle of which are still remaining. The statue must have been of a gigantic size; to have appeared of a man's proportion at so great a height.

ALEXANDRIA, fourth edition (1800–10).

Disagreement as to the Height of Mt. Etna

Ætna, (in the Itineraries *Æthna*, supposed from αἴθω, "to burn"; according to Bochart, from *Athuna*, a furnace, or *Ætuna*, darkness), now *Monte Gibello*: a vulcano or burning mountain of Sicily, situated in lat. 38° N. long. 15° E.

This mountain, famous from the remotest antiquity, both for its bulk and terrible eruptions, stands in the eastern part of the island, in a very extensive plain, called *Val Demoni*, from the notion of its being inhabited by devils, who torment the spirits of the damned in the bowels of this vulcano.

Concerning the dimensions of mount Ætna, we can scarce extract any thing consistent, even from the accounts of the latest and most ingenious travellers. Pindar, who lived about 435 years before Christ, calls it the *Pillar of Heaven*, on account of its great height. All modern [late 18th-century] writers likewise agree, that this mountain is very high, and very large; but differ excessively both as to its height and magnitude: some making it no less than twelve miles high, others eight, others six, some four, while Mr. Brydone, and Sir William Hamilton, who lately ascended to its highest summit, reduce its height to little more than two miles [10,560 ft.]; nay, by some it is reduced to 10,036 feet, somewhat less than two miles. No less remarkable are the differences concerning its circumference: some making it only 60 miles round, others 100; and Signior Recupero, from whom Mr. Brydone had his information in this respect, affirms it to be no less than 183 miles in circuit.

We are sorry to detract from the merit of Mr. Brydone, or to involve in obscurity what he hath been at so much pains to elucidate; but every person who compares the account of mount Ætna's circumference, given by Signior Recupero, and to which Mr. Brydone seems to have assented, with its apparent circumference on the map prefixed to that gentleman's tour through Sicily and Malta, must at once be struck with the prodigious disparity. Indeed, it is plain, that, in the map, the geographer hath not left room for any such mountain; nor can we help thinking, that, by comparing the distances of some of the Sicilian towns from one another, Signior Recupero's dimensions will be found enormously exaggerated.—Certain it is, that there the geographer hath placed Catania, which stands at the foot of mount Ætna, on one side, no more than 28 miles from the most distant point of the river Alcantara, which forms the boundary on the opposite side; so that a circle, whose radius is 14 or 15 miles, must encompass as much space as we can possibly think is occupied by the basis of mount Ætna. Thus we will reduce the circumference of this famous mountain to between 80 and 90 miles; and even when we do so, it must still be acknowledged to be very great.

ÆTNA, second edition (1777–83). [The 1963 printing of the *Encyclopaedia Britannica* in its article on Mount Etna states "the highest point varies above 10,500 ft. and tends to decrease (10,870 ft. in 1861; 10,758 ft. in 1900; 10,705 ft. in 1950). . . . It covers approximately 500 sq. mi. and has a base circumference of about 90 mi."]

Rural Middlesex

The prospects in the southern division of the county of Middlesex, from the level nature of its surface, are not distinguished by extent or variety; and the eye is only relieved from the fatigue of uniformity, by the numerous buildings, plantations, gardens, and the rich verdure of productive grass fields. Even in the more hilly parts of the county the prospects are far less impressive than those upon the opposite banks of the Thames, or those which are to be seen upon the borders of that river before it enters Middlesex. The best prospects of a rural kind are from the range of hills stretching from Pinner, Stanmore, Elstree, Totteridge, and Barnet, to the forest scenery of Enfield Chace. The Hill of Harrow, a projection from this ridge, is one of the highest points; and the whole of the richly-cultivated valley of Middlesex is comprehended in the view from it.

MIDDLESEX, supplement to the fourth, fifth and sixth editions (1816–24).

The Astonishing Growth of Brighton into a Town of Luxury and Fashion

Brighthelmstone, or Brighton, is a town on the sea-coast, in the hundred of Whalesbone and rape of Lewes, in the county of Sussex. The growth of this place is one of those manifestations of the progress of wealth and the increased power of gratification in this kingdom, which on reflection cannot fail to excite astonishment. This town, a small fishing place till 1784, with neither commerce nor manufacture, and with no peculiar advantages even for sea-bathing, which formed the only pretext for visiting it, has, by the mere force of fashion acting upon rapidly-augmented wealth, grown up to be a city almost of palaces, exhibiting a display of every comfort and even luxury, and containing a population of more than 40,000 persons. It is built under the shelter of the South-down Hills, which protect it from the northern and eastern blasts, and hence it is as much a place of resort for the idle, the invalid, and the mere fashionist, in the winter, as it was at its first establishment in the summer season. Magnificent squares and parades have been built, which have speedily found occupants; the embellishments have kept pace with their growth; churches and chapels have been erected to supply religious aid to all sects and all tastes; hotels, club-houses, and other establishments, have been formed for purposes of amusement; carriages and horses are in readiness equal to the demand for them; and every necessary, every accommodation, and almost every luxury, may be found in the markets, the shops, and the repositories. By means of steam-boats it has become one of the passages to France, and from thence the inhabitants can obtain supplies of fruit, vegetables, game, poultry, and other articles at reasonable rates. In addition to other inducements, a German institution for producing all the waters of the most celebrated medicinal springs on the Continent has, at much expense, and with very great scientific skill, been constructed. A new town has been built or is building, called Kemp Town, to contain houses of a large kind, sufficient for ten thousand more inhabitants. According to the government census, the population amounted in 1801 to 7339, in 1811 to 12,012, and in 1821 to 24,429; but the greatest proportional increase has been since the last of these years.

BRIGHTHELMSTONE, seventh edition (1830–42).

Iron Bridges

We have now arrived at an epoch in civil engineering, which at once enlarged tenfold its sphere of action, and rendered impossible all reference to experience or precedent; and the arch and the beam, as well as every other established principle of construction, underwent, with miraculous rapidity, entire modification, and their application became wonderfully extended.

Hitherto, bridges had been applied generally to high roads where inclined approaches were of small importance, and in determining the rise of his arch, the engineer selected any headway he thought proper, while every other consideration was similarly made subsidiary to the problem of constructing the bridge

The calcar is divided into three parts, each vaulted. The glass, or working, furnace (B), divided into two, the upper half (F) for annealing or cooling and the lower with mouths D (with movable covers) of the main glass furnace. The lowest vault, or crown (C), holds the fire. From GLASS, second edition (1777–83).

itself, and the completion of a single large bridge was an epoch in engineering history. On the introduction of railways, hundreds of roads, rivers, and valleys had at once to be spanned with level roads. Time was as important an element as economy or durability in the erection of these structures, while every conceivable difficulty arose from their limited headway, their bad foundations, their oblique directions, or their gigantic dimensions. Navigable waters, as well as crowded thoroughfares, had now to be crossed without interference with existing traffic, and the ponderous locomotive dashed over these new and hastily constructed works, instead of the quiet team. The arch was evidently at once inapplicable to the bulk of such requirements; new principles of construction became imperative, and the beam, with all its numerous modifications, at once superseded the iron arch as completely as the locomotive did the stage coach.

IRON BRIDGES, eighth edition (1853–60). By Robert Stephenson (1803–59), the great civil engineer and only son of George Stephenson.

Installation of Gas-Lighting in Britain

It might have been interesting, in a statistical point of view, to have laid before our readers an account of the extent to which gas-lighting has been carried throughout the kingdom [the first public installation of gas-lighting was made in 1807, in London]; but in a matter which is still in progress, it is not easy to procure documents that would be applicable to any particular period of time. At the close of the year 1822, it appears, by the report of Sir William Congreve, that the capital vested in the gas-works of the metropolis amounted then to about a million sterling; while the pipes, connected with the various establishments, embraced an extent of upwards of a hundred and fifty miles. So rapid, indeed, has been the progress of this new mode of illumination, that, in the course of a few years after it was first introduced, it was adopted by all the principal towns in the kingdom, for lighting streets, as well as shops and public edifices. In private houses it found its way more slowly, partly from an apprehension, not entirely groundless, of the danger attending the use of it; and partly, from the annoyance which was experienced in many cases, through the careless and imperfect manner, in which the service-pipes were at first fitted up. These inconveniences have been, in a great measure, if not wholly removed, by a more enlarged knowledge of the management of gas; and at present there are few private houses, in large towns, which are not either partially, or entirely lighted up by it.

GAS-LIGHT, seventh edition (1830–42). By Adam Anderson (d. 1846), physicist and professor of natural philosophy at St. Andrews university.

Cotton Manufacture

As the successive mechanical inventions which we have described came to be applied to the manufacture, they changed the principle of production, and made what till then had been nearly wholly a product of labour, become [by the 1830s] almost entirely a product of capital. Important results flowed from this change. It enabled Great Britain, the principal holder of these machines, to become the furnisher of a commodity, which up to that time had been brought at a great expense from India. It further enabled her to reduce its cost, and render what till then had been accessible only to the rich, and of limited sale, an article of general wear. During the long struggle which took place between machinery and hand-labour, this country continued to be the nearly exclusive possessor of the machines by which the reduction of cost was effected. Having in consequence, in a great measure, a monopoly of the supply, she was enabled to reap that harvest of prosperity which so unusual a combination of circumstances was calculated to produce. An improvement in the condition of every class of the community followed the advance of the manufacture. The progressive extension of the use of machinery, in place of lessening the demand for labour, as was at first dreaded, had the effect of increasing it to an extraordinary degree. There was a constantly growing want of hands to be employed in aid of the new machinery, and in the new branches of manufacture to which it gave birth. The wages of labour in consequence rose, at

first moderately, but afterwards extensively; and the rise, having pervaded every description of employment, not only gave the whole labouring class in this country a command of the comforts of life, but brought within their reach many little luxuries to which they were formerly unaccustomed. The condition of the higher classes of the community experienced a corresponding advance, the population rapidly increased, and an enlarged consumption of the products of the soil took place, in consequence of the improved circumstances, as well as of the augmented numbers, of the people. More grain, more butcher-meat, were used; and an additional quantity of corn was required for the horses employed in the transport of commodities, in the conveyance of passengers, and in the operations of husbandry. All these causes gave a stimulus to agriculture, and produced a change in that important branch of industry, not less remarkable than that which was simultaneously taking place in manufactures.

But having reached this high state of prosperity, it may be asked, what security have we that we shall be able to maintain our pre-eminence in this manufacture, now that other countries, over which we possess no natural advantage, are using efforts to participate in its benefits?

To this it can only be answered, that the hopes of our being able to preserve our vantage-ground, rest upon our persevering industry, our economy, our great capital, the advanced state of our machinery, our attainments in mechanical knowledge, the benefit we derive from having been long in possession of the business, and the better acquaintance with the minutiae of its processes. The lead we have thus taken we think it probable we may for a long time be able to maintain; for invention is progressive, and in a manufacture extended like ours, every discovery that is made has the effect to unfold principles leading to other discoveries, or to suggest analogous applications in other departments. Those who conduct the various processes of manufacture, and those employed in the operative part of them, have all their thoughts constantly turned to the means of enlarging the powers of the machines they are in possession of, or to the discovery of others for executing parts of the work still performed by the hand. Besides the mere progress in machinery, there is a progress also in the use of machinery, of contrivances to supply its defects, and of little, undefinable, subsidiary aids, for the furtherance of the work to be done, which contribute to give a vast superiority to those who have been long habituated to the use of it. . . .

The more perfect division of labour and separation of employment which takes place as the use of machinery advances, and the consequent limitation of the worker's attention to a single object, check the expansion of the faculties, and prevent that growth of intelligence in this class, which under a more general employment of their powers might be expected. Another evil of a similar nature, but attended perhaps with more serious consequences, is produced by manufactures when they have arrived at this state, namely, the employment of children in factories, by which these young creatures are withdrawn from their parents and homes before they have received the elements of education, or can have acquired domestic or moral habits.

In noticing these evils, however, we must recollect that the state of manufacture which gives birth to them is not an optional one, nor the production of regulation or institution, but has grown up in the progress of the arts of industry, prosecuted by an intelligent people. Although, therefore, it is our duty, in as far as we can, to correct their effects, we must lay our account with being exposed to them, so long as men are allowed to pursue their individual interest, by whatever fair means they conceive likely to accomplish their object.

To remedy in as far as possible the interruption to education, schools have been established in many of the factories, in which the children are instructed gratis in reading and writing. An institution of this kind we consider it to be the interest of the proprietor of every work to provide. In the mean time, something is done to supply the deficiency of this provision by Sunday schools, which have been generally established in most of the manufacturing towns. In these, the children are not only taught to read, but are also instructed in the principles of religion, and in a knowledge of their moral duties.

In the year 1800, a course of lectures was given for the first time in Glasgow, in the Andersonian Institution, to the mechanics and working classes, with the view of affording them instruction in the science of their different employments. . . .

So important does this species of instruction appear to us in the circumstances of this country, where so much depends on our being able to keep the lead which we have got in mechanical invention and discovery, that we think it worthy of consideration in a national point of view, whether, in the appointment of our parochial schoolmasters, it might not be declared indispensable that they should be qualified to teach the first principles of mechanics and chemistry.

With the stores of the raw material of machinery which we possess, might we not, with a proper training of our people, become machine-makers for all the nations who are less favourably circumstanced? The advantage of being able to occupy such ground would be incalculable.

COTTON MANUFACTURE, seventh edition (1830–42). By Dugald Bannatyne.

Baldness: Some Supposed Cures

In cases where the baldness is total, a quantity of the finest burdock roots are to be bruised in a marble mortar, and then boiled in white wine until there remains only as much as will cover them. This liquor, carefully strained off, is said to cure baldness, by washing the head every night with some of it warm. A ley made by boiling ashes of vine branches in common water is also recommended with this intention. A fresh cut onion, rubbed on the part until it be red and itch, is likewise said to cure baldness.

A multitude of such remedies are everywhere to be found in the works of Valescus de Taranta, Rondeletius, Hollerius, Trincavellius, Celsus, Senertay, and other practical physicians.

ALOPECIA, fourth edition (1800–10).

Rosemary and Its Uses

Rosmarinus, in botany, a genus of the diandria monogynia class. The corolla is unequal, and the upper lip of it is split into two segments; the filaments are long, crooked, and simple. There is but one species, viz. the officinalis, a native of Spain.

Rosemary is a very valuable cephalic, and is good in all disorders of the nerves, and in hysteric and hypochondriac diseases. It is good in palsies, apoplexies, epilepsies, and vertigoes.

ROSMARINUS, first edition (1768–71).

Mustard-Seed and Its Uses

Sinapi, in botany, a genus of the tetradynamia siliquosa class. The calix is open; the petals have straight ungues; and there is a nectarious gland between the short stamina and the pistillum, and between the long stamina and the calix. There are ten species, three of them natives of Britain, viz. the nigra, or common mustard; the alba, or white mustard; and the arvensis, or wild mustard.

Mustard-seed is an attenuant and resolvent in a very high degree; it warms the stomach, and excites an appetite; but its principal medicinal use is external in sinapisms, applications made to certain parts when irritation is intended, but not blistering. It is usually mixed with horse-radish root, and other ingredients of the same kind, for this purpose.

SINAPI, first edition (1768–71).

Zedoary and Its Uses

Zedoary, in the materia medica, a root, the several pieces of which differ so much from one another in shape, that they have been divided into two kinds, as if two different things, under the names of the long and round zedoary, being only the several parts of the same root.

Zedoary is to be chosen fresh, sound, and hard, in large pieces; it matters not as to shape, whether long or round; of a smooth surface, and of a sort of fatty appearance within, too hard to be bitten by the teeth, and of the briskest smell that may be; such as is friable, dusty and worm-eaten, is to be rejected.

Zedoary, both of the long and round kind, is brought us from China; and we find by the Arabians, that they also had it from the same place. The round tubera are less frequent than the long, and some people have therefore supposed them the produce of a different and more rare plant; but this is not so probable as that the general form of the root is long, and the round tubera are only lusus naturae, and less frequent in it.

Zedoary, distilled with common water, affords a thick and dense essential oil, which soon concretes of itself into a kind of camphor, and on this oil its virtues principally depend. It is a sudorific, and is much recommended by some in fevers, especially of the malignant kinds. It is also given with success as an expectorant in all disorders of the breast, arising from a tough phlegm, which it powerfully incides and attenuates; it is also good against flatulences, and in the cholic; it strengthens the stomach, and assists digestion; and, finally, is given with success in nervous cases of all kinds.

ZEDOARY, first edition (1768-71).

Alleged Virtues of Dew

The dew of heaven has always been regarded as a fluid of the purest and most translucid nature. Hence it was celebrated for that abstergent property which, according to the vulgar persuasion, enables it to remove all spots and stains, and to impart to the skin the bloom and freshness of virgin beauty. Like the elixir of later times, it was conceived to possess the power of extending the duration of human life; and Ammianus Marcellinus ascribes the longevity and robust health of mountaineers, in comparison with the inhabitants of the plains, chiefly to the frequent aspersion of dew on their gelid bodies. Dew was also employed as a most powerful agent, in all their operations, by the alchemists; some of whom pretended that is possessed such a subtle and penetrating efficacy, as to be capable of dissolving gold itself. Following out the same idea, the people of remote antiquity fancied that the external application of dew had some virtue in correcting any disposition to corpulence. The ladies of those days, anxious to preserve their fine forms, procured this celestial wash, by exposing clothes or fleeces of wool to the humifaction of the night. It was likewise imagined, that grasshoppers feed wholly on dew, and owe their lean features perhaps to such spare diet.

DEW, supplement to the fourth, fifth and sixth editions (1816-24).

Noah's Ark

The dimensions of the ark, as given by Moses, are 300 cubits in length, 50 in breadth, and 30 in height; which some have thought too scanty, considering the number of things it was to contain; and hence an argument has been drawn against the authority of the relation. To solve this difficulty, many of the ancient fathers and the modern critics have been put to very miserable shifts: But Buteo and Kircher have proved geometrically, that taking the common cubit of a foot and a half, the ark was abundantly sufficient for all the animals supposed to be lodged in it. Snellius computes the ark to have been above half an acre in area. Father Lamy shows, that it was 110 feet longer than the church

Noah's ark floating on the waters of the deluge. From ARK, *fourth edition (1800-10).*

of St. Mary at Paris, and 64 feet narrower: and if so, it must have been longer than St. Paul's church in London, from west to east, and broader than that church is high in the inside, and 54 feet of our measure in height; and Dr. Arbuthnot computes it to have been 81062 tons. . . .

By the description Moses gives of the ark, it appears to have been divided into three stories, each ten cubits or 15 feet high; and it is agreed on, as most probable, that the lowest story was for the beasts, the middle for the food, and the upper for the birds, with Noah and his family; each story being subdivided into different apartments, stalls, etc. though Josephus, Philo, and other commentators, add a kind of fourth story under all the rest; being, as it were, the hold of the vessel, to contain the ballast and receive the filth and faeces of so many animals: but F. Calmet thinks, that what is here reckoned a story, was no more than what is called the *keel* of ships, and served only for a conservatory of fresh water.

ARK, fourth edition (1800–10).

Duration of Original Innocence

How long our first parents retained their innocence, we are nowhere told. Many assert that they fell on the very first day of their creation. But Moses mentions so many transactions on that day, as must have engrossed the whole of their attention, and prevented them from falling into such temptations as arise from indolence and want of reflection. Besides, if, in such circumstances as they were placed, they could not refrain from an open violation of the Divine law for the space of one day, it would bespeak a deceitfulness of heart in them greater than in most of their posterity.

ANTEDILUVIANS, fourth edition (1800–10).

Astronomy

It is not to be imagined that all the stars are placed in one concave surface, so as to be equally distant from us; but that they are scattered at immense distances from one another through unlimited space. So that there may be as great a distance between any two neighbouring stars, as between our sun and those which are nearest to him. Therefore an observer, who is nearest any fixed star, will look upon it alone as a real sun; and consider the rest as so many shining points, placed at equal distances from him in the firmament.

By the help of telescopes we discover thousands of stars which are invisible to the naked eye; and the better our glasses are, still the more become visible; so that no limits can be set either to their number or their distances.

The sun appears very bright and large in comparison of the fixed stars, because we keep constantly near the sun, in comparison of our immense distance from the stars. For a spectator, placed as near to any star as we are to the sun, would see that star a body as large and bright as the sun appears to us: and a spectator, as far distant from the sun as we are from the stars, would see the sun as small as we see a star, divested of all its circumvolving planets; and would reckon it one of the stars in numbering them. . . .

Some of the stars, particularly Arcturus, have been observed to change their places above a minute of a degree with respect to others. But whether this be owing to any real motion in the stars themselves, must require the observations of many ages to determine. If our solar system changeth its place, with regard to absolute space, this must in process of time occasion an apparent change in the distances of the stars from each other: and in such a case, the places of the nearest stars to us being more affected than those which are very remote, their relative positions must seem to alter, though the stars themselves were really immoveable. On the other hand, if our own system be at rest, and any of the stars in real motion, this must vary their positions; and the more so, the nearer they are to us, or the swifter their motions are, or the more proper the direction of their motion is for our perception.

ASTRONOMY, first edition (1768–71).

Aether

Aether, the name of an imaginary fluid, supposed by several authors, both ancient and modern, to be the cause of gravity, heat, light, muscular motion, sensation, and, in a word, of every phaenomenon in nature. . . .

It must indeed be acknowledged, that there is a propensity in the human mind, which, unless it be properly restrained, has a direct tendency both to corrupt science, and to retard our progress in it. Not contented with the examination of objects which readily fall within the sphere of our observation, we feel a strong desire to account for things which, from their very nature, must, and ever will, elude our researches. Even Sir Isaac Newton himself was not proof against this temptation. It was not enough that he had discovered the nature of light and colours, the application of gravity to the motions of the heavenly bodies, *etc.* he must go further, and attempt to assign the cause of gravity itself. But, how does he proceed in this matter? Not in the way of experiment, which had led him to his former discoveries, but in the way of conjecture, which will never lead any man to truth. He had recourse to a subtile elastic aether, not much different from that of the ancients, and by it accounted for every thing he did not know, such as the cause of gravitation, muscular motion, sensation, *etc.*

Notwithstand the reputation of Sir Isaac, philosophers have generally looked upon this attempt as the foible of a great man, or, at least, as the most useless part of his works; and accordingly peruse it rather as a dream or a romance, than as having any connection with science. But we are sorry to find, that some late attempts have been made to revive this doctrine of aether, particularly in a dissertation *De ortu animalium caloris*.

AETHER, third edition (1788–97).

Electricity

Electricity, in general, signifies [*c.* 1790] the operations of a very subtile fluid, in most cases invisible, but which sometimes becomes the object of our sight and other senses, discovering itself to be one of the chief agents employed in producing the phenomena of nature. . . .

For some time, the science of electricity seems to have been at a stand. Numberless improvements indeed have been made upon what was before discovered, but scarce any new thing hath been added. The only thing which can be properly reckoned a new discovery is that of the *electrophorus* by Signior Volta an Italian; which on many accounts may be reckoned the most surprising machine hitherto invented. . . .

The first [electrical machine] which may be mentioned is that described by Dr. Priestley in his history of electricity; which, on account of its extensive use, may be deservedly called a *universal electrical machine.*— The basis consists of two oblong boards, which are placed in a situation parallel to one another, about four inches asunder, and kept in that position by two pieces of wood adapted for the purpose. These boards, when set horizontally on a table, and the lowermost of them fixed with iron cramps, form the support of two perpendicular pillars of baked wood, and of the rubber of the machine. One of the pillars, together with the spring supporting the rubber, slides in a groove *a*, which reaches almost the whole length of the upper board; and, by means of a screw, may be placed at any required distance from the pillar *b*, which is fixed, being put through a mortice in the upper board,

and fastened to the lower. In these two pillars are several holes for the admittance of the spindles of different globes; and as they may be situated at any distance from one another, they may be adapted to receive not only globes, but cylinders and spheroids of different sizes. "In this machine (says Dr. Priestley), more than one globe or cylinder may be used at once, by fixing one above the other in the different holes of the pillars; and by adapting to each a proper pulley, they may be whirled all at once, to increase the electricity." But this construction has one capital defect, that rubbers cannot be conveniently applied; so that the power of several globes put together in this manner, though greater than one, is by no means equal to what it would be if the power of them all taken singly were untied.

The rubber ought to be made as above directed. It is supported by a socket which receives the cylindrical axis of a round and flat piece of glass or baked wood *g*, the opposite part of which is inserted into the socket of a bent steel spring *h*. These parts are easily separated, so that the rubber, or the piece of wood that serves to insulate it, may be changed at pleasure. The spring admits of a twofold alteration of position; being capable of either slipping along the groove, or moving in the contrary direction, the groove being wider than the screw that fastens the spring, so as to give it every desirable position with regard to the globe or cylinder; and it is besides furnished with a screw which makes it press harder or lighter as the operator chooses. The wheel of this machine is fixed to the table at *e*, and has several grooves for admitting more strings than one, in case that two or three globes or cylinders are used at a time; and as it is disengaged from the frame of the machine, the latter may be screwed at different distances from the former, and so would be suited to the variable length of the string. The chain connected with the rubber at *n* is for making a communication

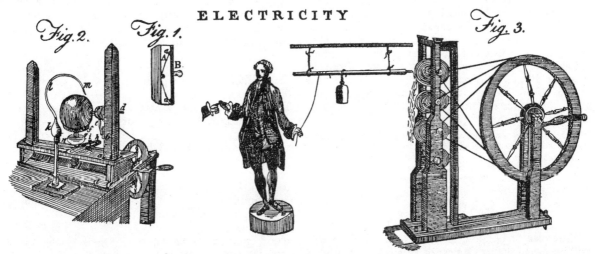

Figs. 1 and 2 show the machine described by Dr. Priestley and Fig. 3 Dr. Watson's machine. From ELECTRICITY, *third edition (1788–97).*

with the table, when insulation is not wanted. The prime conductor is made of copper, hollow, and in the form of a pear; having its neck placed upwards, and its bottom, or rounded part *k*, placed on a stand of glass or baked wood. An arched wire *l* proceeds from its neck, having an open ring at its end, in which some small pointed wires *m* are hung, that by playing lightly on the globe or cylinder collect the electric fluid.

Fig. 3 shows a machine contrived by Dr. Watson. ELECTRICITY, third edition (1788–97).

The Scientist's Need of Intercommunication

Frequent communication of ideas, and a regular method of keeping up such communication, are evidently essential to works in which great labour and industry are to be employed, and to which much time must necessarily be devoted; when the philosopher must not always sit quietly in his cabinet, but must examine nature with his own eyes, and be present in the work-shop of the mechanic, or the laboratory of the chemist. These operations are facilitated by the institutions now referred to, which, therefore, are of more importance to the physical sciences than to the other branches of knowledge. They who cultivate the former are also fewer in number, and being, of course, farther separated, are less apt to meet together in the common intercourse of the world. The historian, the critic, the poet, finds everywhere men who can enter in some degree at least into his pursuits, who can appreciate his merit, and derive pleasure from his writings or his conversation. The mathematician, the astronomer, the mechanician, sees few men who have much sympathy with his pursuits, or who do not look with indifference on the objects which he pursues. The *world*, to him, consists of a few individuals, by the censures or approbation of whom the public opinion must be finally determined; with them it is material that he should have more frequently intercourse than could be obtained by casual rencounter; and he feels that the society of men engaged in pursuits similar to his own, is a necessary *stimulus* to his exertions. Add to this, that such societies become centers in which information concerning facts is collected from all quarters. For all these reasons, the greatest benefit has resulted from the scientific institutions which, since the middle of the seventeenth century, have become so numerous in Europe.

DISSERTATION: *exhibiting a general view of the Progress of Mathematical and Physical Science,* supplement to the fourth, fifth and sixth editions (1816–24). By John Playfair (1748–1819), mathematician and geologist, professor of mathematics and later of natural philosophy at Edinburgh university.

London: A Sketch with Statistics

The plan of London, in its present state [*c.* 1790], will in many instances appear to very moderate judges to be as injudicious a disposition as can easily be conceived for a city of trade and commerce, on the borders of so noble a river as the Thames. The wharfs and quays on its banks are extremely mean and inconvenient; and the want of regularity and uniformity in the streets of the city of London, and the mean avenues to many parts of it, are also circumstances that greatly lessen the grandeur of its appearance. Many of the churches and other public buildings are likewise thrust up in corners, in such a manner as might tempt foreigners to believe that they were designed to be concealed. The improvements of the city of London for some years past have, however, been very great; and the new streets which are numerous, are in general more spacious, and built with greater regularity and elegance.

The very elegant and necessary method of paving and enlightening the streets is also felt in the most sensible manner by all ranks and degrees of people. The roads are continued for several miles around upon the same model; and, exclusive of lamps regularly placed on each side at short distances, are rendered more secure by watchmen stationed within call of each other. Nothing can appear more brilliant than those lights when viewed at a distance, especially where the roads run across; and even the principal streets, such as Pall Mall, New Bond street, Oxford-street, &c. convey an idea of elegance and grandeur. . . .

There are also in and near this city 100 alms-houses, about 20 hospitals and infirmaries, 3 colleges, 10 public prisons, 15 flesh-markets; one market for live cattle; two markets more particularly for herbs; and 23 other markets for corn, coals, hay, &c., 15 inns of court, 27 public squares, besides those within single buildings, as the Temple, &c.; 3 bridges, 55 halls for companies, 8 public schools, called free-schools; and 131 charity-schools, which provide education for 5034 poor children; 207 inns, 447 taverns, 551 coffee-houses, 5975 alehouses; 1000 hackney-coaches; 400 ditto chairs; 7000 streets, lanes, courts, and allays, and 150,000 dwelling-houses, containing, as has been already observed, about 1,000,000 inhabitants; who, according to a moderate estimate, are supposed to consume the following provisions weekly.

	£	s.	d.
1000 Bullocks, at £6 a-piece —	6000	0	0
6000 Sheep, at 12s. a-piece —	3600	0	0
2000 Calves, at £1 4s. a-piece —	2400	0	0
3000 Lambs, at 8s. a-piece, for six months —	1200	0	0
1500 Hogs in pork and bacon, at 20s. for six months	1500	0	0
2000 Pigs at 2s. 6d. a-piece —	250	0	0
1000 Turkies, at 3s. 6d. a-piece, for six months —	175	0	0
1000 Geese, at 2s. 6d. a-piece, for six months —	125	0	0
2000 Capons, at 1s. 8d. a-piece —	166	13	2
500 Dozens of Chickens at 9s. per dozen —	225	0	0
4300 Ducks, at 9d. a-piece —	161	5	0

1500 Dozen of rabbits, at 7*s. per*
dozen, for eight months — 525 0 0
2000 Dozen of pigeons, at 2*s. per*
dozen, for eight months — 200 0 0
700 Dozen of wild-fowl, of several
sorts, for six months — 250 0 0
In salt and fresh fish, at 1*d.* a-day, for
half a million of people for one
week — 14,510 6 8
In bread of all sorts, white and
brown at 1*d.* a-day, for one
million of people for a week — 29,166 13 4
300 Tons of wine, of all sorts, at
£50 a ton, one sort with another,
for one week — 15,000 0 0
In milk, butter, cheese, &c. at 1*d.* a
day, for a million of people for a
week — 29,166 13 4
In fruit of all sorts, at one farthing
a-day, for a million of people for
a week — 7291 13 4
In eggs of hens, ducks, geese, &c. at
half a farthing a-day, for a
million of people for a week — 3645 16 4
In beer and ale, strong and small, at
2*d.* a day, for a million of people
for a week — 58,333 6 8
In sugar, plums, and spice, and all
sorts of grocery, at a halfpenny
a-day, for a million of people for
a week — 14,583 6 8
In wheat flour for pies and pud-
dings, oatmeal and rice, &c. at
half a farthing a-day for a million
of people for a week — 3645 16 8
In salt, oil, vinegar, capers, olives,
and other sauces, at half a farthing a-day for a million of people
for a week — 3645 16 8
In roots and herbs of all sorts, both
for food and physic, at half a
farthing a-day, for a million of
people for a week — 3645 16 8
In sea-coal, charcoal, candles, and
fire-wood, of all sorts, at 1*d.* a-
day, for a million of people for a
week — 29,166 13 4
In paper of all sorts (a great quantity
being used in printing) quills,
pens, ink, and wax, at a farthing
a-day for a million of people for
a week — 7291 13 4
In tobacco, pipes, and snuff, at half
a farthing a-day, for a million of
people for a week — 3643 16 8
In clothing, as linen and woollen,
men, women and children, shoes,
stockings, &c. at 3*s.* 6*d. per* week,
for a million of people for a
week — 175,000 0 0

Expences for horse-meat, in hay,
oats, beans, 1000 load of hay a-
week, at 40*s,* a-load, comes to
£2000 in oats and beans the like
value, £2000 which is in all for
one week 4000 0 0
Cyder, mum, brandy, strong waters,
coffee, chocolate, tea, &c. at 1*d.*
a-day, for a million of people for
one week — 29,166 13 4

LONDON, third edition (1788-97).

Portrait of Samuel Johnson

The influence exercised by his conversation, directly upon those with whom he lived, and indirectly on the whole literary world, was altogether without a parallel. His colloquial talents were indeed of the highest order. He had strong sense, quick discernment, wit, humour, immense knowledge of literature, and of life and an infinite store of curious anecdotes. As respected style, he spoke far better than he wrote. Every sentence which dropped from his lips was as correct in structure as the most nicely balanced period of his magazine the *Rambler*. But in his talk there were no pompous triads, and little more than a fair proportion of words in *osity* and *ation*. All was simplicity, ease, and vigour. He uttered his short, weighty, and pointed sentences with a power of voice, and a justness and energy of emphasis, of which the effect was rather increased than diminished by the rollings of his huge form, and by the asthmatic gaspings and puffings in which the peals of his eloquence generally ended. Nor did the laziness which made him unwilling to sit down to his desk prevent him from giving instruction or entertainment orally. To discuss questions of taste, of learning, of casuistry, in language so exact and so forcible that it might have been printed without the alteration of a word, was to him no exertion, but a pleasure. He loved, as he said, to fold his legs and have his talk out. He was ready to bestow the overflowings of his full mind on anybody who would start a subject, on a fellow-passenger in a stage coach, or on the person who sate at the same table with him in an eating-house. But his conversation was nowhere so brilliant and striking as when he was surrounded by a few friends, whose abilities and knowledge enabled them, as he once expressed it, to send him back every ball that he threw. . . .

Boswell's book has done for him more than the best of his own books could do. The memory of other authors is kept alive by their works. But the memory of Johnson keeps many of his works alive. The old philosopher is still among us in the brown coat with the metal buttons and the shirt which ought to be at wash, blinking, puffing, rolling his head, drumming with his fingers, tearing his meat like a tiger, and swallowing his tea in oceans. No human being who has been more than seventy years in the grave is so well known to us. And it is but just to say that our intimate acquaintance with what he would himself have called the anfractuosities of his intellect and of his temper, serves only to strengthen our conviction that he was both a great and a good man.

JOHNSON, SAMUEL, eighth edition (1853–60). By Lord Macaulay (1800–59), historian, essayist and politician.

Joseph Addison

Mr. Tyers, in "An historical Essay on Mr. Addison," printed, but not published, has mentioned some facts concerning him, with which we were not before acquainted. These are, That he was laid out for dead as soon as he was born: that, when he addressed his verses on the English poets to Henry Sacheverell, he courted that gentleman's sister: that, whenever Jacob Tonson came to him for the Spectator, Bayle's French Historical and Critical Dictionary lay always open before him: that upon his return to England, after his travels, he discharged some old debts he had contracted at Oxford, with the generosity of good interest: that he was put into plentiful circumstances by the death of a brother in the East Indies: that, having received encouragement from a married lady, of whom he had been formerly enamoured, he had the integrity to resist the temptation: that he refused a gratification of a three hundred pounds bank-note, and afterwards of a diamond-ring of the same value, from a Major Dunbar, whom he had endeavoured to serve in Ireland by his interest with Lord Sunderland: and that his daughter by lady Warwick is still alive and unmarried, residing at Bilton near Rugby, and possessing an income of more than twelve hundred a year.

The anecdote which follows was told by the late Dr. Birch. Addison and Mr. Temple Stanyan were very intimate. In the familiar conversations which passed between them, they were accustomed freely to dispute each others opinions. Upon some occasion, Mr. Addison lent Stanyan five hundred pounds. After this, Mr. Stanyan behaved with a timid reserve, deference and respect; not conversing with the same freedom as formerly, or canvassing his friend's sentiments. This gave great uneasiness to Mr. Addison. One day they happened to fall on a subject, on which Mr. Stanyan had always been used strenuously to oppose his opinion. But, even upon this occasion, he gave way to what his friend advanced, without interposing his own view of the matter. This hurt Mr. Addison so much, that he said to Mr. Stanyan, "Either contradict me, or pay me the money."

ADDISON, third edition (1788–97).

Portrait of Kant

In his person, Kant [the German Idealist philosopher; 1724–1804] was rather below the middle stature, of a slender and delicate form, and with a very narrow and flat chest. His bodily frame, indeed, did

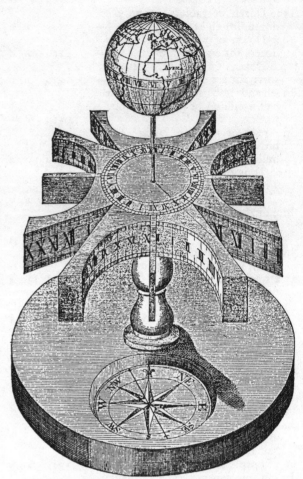

An universal dial, shewing the hours of the day by a terrestrial globe, and by the shadows of several gnomons, at the same time: together with all the places of the earth which are then enlightened by the sun; and those to which the sun is then rising, or on the meridian, or setting. From DIAL, *first edition (1768–71).*

not seem to promise longevity; nor would he, in all probability, have attained so great an age, had not his constitution been preserved by his regular and temperate mode of living. In his external appearance, strangers found nothing prepossessing, or indicative of any uncommon talents; on the contrary, his features are represented by a gentleman who visited him at Koningsberg, as "a reproach to physiognomy." Others, however, describe his countenance as full of dignity, and expressive of benevolence. His natural disposition was cheerful and social; and his manners polite and affable. He exhibited none of that awkwardness, or reserve, which is frequently generated, or increased by habits of recluse meditation, and which is often thought to be characteristic of the scholar and man of science. He loved company, and was both inquisitive himself, and fond of communicating his own knowledge and opinions upon all subjects. There was nothing, however trifling it might appear, at first sight, which did not suggest to his mind some interesting reflections; and he could talk as fluently with a lady on the *minutiæ* of female dress, the mysteries of the kitchen, or the common occurrences of the day, as he could with a philosopher on the most abstruse points of science.

Kant's intellectual faculties were of a high order. He had a wonderful power of reflection,·which enabled him to unfold the most abstruse principles, and to pursue, in his own mind, a long train of conclusions. He possessed great quickness of observation, and clearness of conception; insomuch that, in conversation, he could describe any object which he had seen, or of which he had read, with admirable precision and accuracy. His memory was exceedingly retentive. He kept no library, but made a contract with a bookseller to send him all new publications, which he perused, and afterwards returned; and the knowledge thus acquired he had always at his command. The most remarkable feature in the moral character of Kant, was an utter abhorrence of every species of falsehood, however innocent, and a love of perfect honesty and sincerity, in word and action, flowing no less from his natural disposition, than from those high principles which he had early imbibed, of the value of truth, and the dignity of man. In this respect he was ever consistent with himself; and the whole tenor of his long life may be regarded as a practical commentary on his writings, and an exemplification of his moral maxims.

KANT (IMMANUEL), supplement to the fourth, fifth and sixth editions (1816-24). By John Colquhoun, fellow of the Royal Society of Edinburgh.

Beauty

Beauty,—that property in objects by which they are recommended to the power or faculty of TASTE—the reverse of Ugliness—the primary or most general object of love or admiration.

It is easy enough to understand how the sight of a picture or statue should affect us·nearly in the same way as the sight of the original: nor is it much more difficult to conceive, how the sight of a cottage should give us something of the same feeling as the sight of a peasant's family; and the aspect of a town raise many of the same ideas as the appearance of a multitude of persons. We may begin, therefore, with an example a little more complicated. Take, for instance, the case of a common English landscape—green meadows with fat cattle—canals or navigable rivers—well fenced, well cultivated fields—neat, clean, scattered cottages —humble antique church, with church yard elms, and crossing hedgerows—all seen under bright skies, and in good weather:—There is much Beauty, as every one will acknowledge, in such a scene. But in what does the Beauty consist? Not certainly in the mere mixture of colours and forms; for colours more pleasing, and lines more graceful (according to any theory of grace

that may be preferred), might be spread upon a board, or a painter's pallet, without engaging the eye to a second glance, or raising the least emotion in the mind; —but in the picture of human happiness that is presented to our imaginations and affections,—in the visible and unequivocal signs of comfort, and cheerful and peaceful enjoyment,—and of that secure and successful industry that ensures its continuance,—and of the piety by which it is exalted,—and of the simplicity by which it is contrasted with the guilt and the fever of a city life;—in the images of health and temperance and plenty which it exhibits to every eye,—and in the glimpses which it affords to warmer imaginations, of those primitive or fabulous times, when man was uncorrupted by luxury and ambition, and of those humble retreats in which we still delight to imagine that love and philosophy may find an unpolluted asylum. At all events, however, it is human feeling that excites our sympathy, and forms the object of our emotions. It is man, and man alone, that we see in the beauties of the earth which he inhabits;—or, if a more sensitive and extended sympathy connect us with the lower families of animated nature, and make us rejoice with the lambs that bleat on the uplands, or the cattle that ruminate in the valley, or even with the living plants that drink the bright sun and the balmy air beside them, it is still the idea of enjoyment—of feelings that animate the existence of sentient beings—that calls forth all our emotions, and is the parent of all the Beauty with which we proceed to invest the inanimate creation around us.

. . . there is no such thing as absolute or intrinsic Beauty, and it depends altogether on those associations with which it is thus found to come and to disappear. The accidental or arbitrary relations that may thus be established between natural sympathies or emotions, and external objects, may be either such as occur to whole classes of men, or are confined to particular individuals. Among the former, those that apply to different nations or races of men, are the most important and remarkable; and constitute the basis of those peculiarities by which National Tastes are distinguished. Take, again, for example, the instance of female Beauty,—and think what different and inconsistent standards would be fixed for it in the different regions of the world;—in Africa, in Asia, and in Europe;—in Tartary and in Greece; in Lapland, Patagonia and Circassia. If there was anything absolutely or intrinsically Beautiful, in any of the forms thus distinguished, it is inconceivable that men should differ so outrageously in their conceptions of it.

BEAUTY, supplement to the fourth, fifth and sixth editions (1816-24). By Francis Jeffrey (1773-1850), Scottish judge and editor of the *Edinburgh Review*.

Giotto

Giotto, an ingenious painter, sculptor, and architect of Florence, born in 1276 [the date is disputed, 1266/67? now usually being preferred]. He was the disciple of Cimabue; but far superior to his master in the air of his heads, the attitude of his figures, and in the tone of his colouring; but could not express liveliness in the eyes, tenderness in the flesh, or strength in the muscles of his naked figures. He was principally admired for his works in mosaic; the best of which is over the grand entrance of St. Peter's church at Rome. The observation of Alberti on that piece is, that in the ship of Giotto, the expression of fright and amazement of the disciples at seeing St. Peter walk upon the water is so excellent, that each of them exhibits some characteristic signs of his terror. His death happened in 1336 [Jan. 8, 1337], and the city of Florence honoured his memory with a statue of marble over his tomb.

GIOTTO, second edition (1777-83).

The Royal Academy

As usual, when Reynolds and Hogarth had for ever rescued Britain from all doubt as to her genius, without an academy of any description, a royal academy was founded [1768] to produce more genius, just as had been done all over Europe; and no man equal to Reynolds and Hogarth has since appeared. After the academy was founded at Milan by Leonardo, no genius like his appeared. After that of St. Luke was founded at Rome, Raffaelle and all being dead, no one came forth. After an academy had been founded at Parma, Corregio being gone, nobody appeared. After a national academy was founded at Venice, and royally endowed, genius fled. The same thing happened in Ferrara, Modena, Florence, and Naples; and also in France, Spain, and England. Need further evidence be sought of the uselessness of such institutions? . . .

In consequence of the perpetual complaints from the great body of artists, the government granted a committee in 1836, to examine the cause of the superiority of France in manufacturing design, as well as the condition of high art, and to ascertain if the accusations against the Royal Academy were true or false. Never in the world were the consequences of a monopoly on the perceptions of respectable men so ludicrously developed. The president and body first denied the right of the House of Commons to examine them at all; and when the persuasions of their friends showed them their folly, their appearance before the committee presented a scene never to be forgotten in the history of English painting. On all questions of finance, they proved satisfactorily the honour of their transactions; but on all questions of art more was proved against them than ever had been suspected. The resignation of Reynolds, and the expulsion of Barry; the loss of a million of money to the art on the Waterloo monument, in consequence of their not replying to Lord Castlereagh's committee; their refusal to let the artists also support their exhibition, and have the same opportunities of fitting their works

for the public as at the British Gallery; and, to crown all, their rendering the school of design lately established of no avail to the mechanic, by establishing a law, that the study of the figure is not necessary, for his education, though it was proved that this study at the Lyons academy for mechanics, was the real cause of their superiority to us; are such indisputable evidence against their protestations of sincerity, that it has rendered the nobility and the nation more than suspicious of the truth of all the accusations which have been made against them. . . .

In a word, it is our decided and unprejudiced conviction, that the genius of the British people, will never have fair play or be soundly advanced, till the Royal Academy is removed, or effectually remodelled; and this will be effected either by the positive interference of the queen or the government, or by the rapidly increasing knowledge of the people. If the capital and the provinces were freed from the predominance of those men; if the honours were abolished and the constituencies restored; if the whole national galleries were turned into a great school, with branch schools in the great towns; if the Cartoons were removed to London for the occasional sight of the people, as they might be inclined to drop in; and if a Native Gallery were arranged for the best productions to be purchased as they appeared, and the House of Lords adorned with a series of grand works referring to the British constitution; then would the government do a real good to taste, refined pleasures, and design for manufactures, such as would entitle them to the ever-lasting gratitude of the nation.

PAINTING, eighth edition (1853-60). By Benjamin Robert Haydon (1786-1846), historical painter and writer.

Hogarth's Genius

Hogarth [1697-1764] is in art the first name in the order of time that we have to boast of, and is the greatest comic painter of any age or country. His pictures are not imitations of still life, or mere transcripts of incidental scenes or customs; but powerful moral satires, exposing vice and folly in their most ludicrous points of view, and, with a profound insight into the weak sides of character and manners, in all their tendencies, combinations, and contrasts. His object is not so much "to hold the mirror up to nature," as "to show vice her own feature, scorn her own image." Folly is there seen at the height—the moon is at the full—it is the very error of the time. There is a perpetual collision of eccentricities, a tilt and tournament of absurdities, pampered into all sorts of affectation, airy, extravagant, and ostentatious! Yet he is as little a caricaturist as he is a painter of still life. Criticism has not done him justice, though public opinion has. His works have received a sanction which it would be vain to dispute, in the universal delight and admiration with which they have been regarded, from their first appearance to the present moment. If the quantity of amusement, or of matter for reflection, which they have afforded, is that by which we are to judge of precedence among the intellectual benefactors of mankind, there are perhaps few persons who can put in a stronger claim to our gratitude than Hogarth. . . . Some persons object to the style of Hogarth's pictures, or the class to which they belong. First, Hogarth belongs to no class, or, if he belongs to any, it is to the same class as Fielding, Smollett, Vanbrugh, and Molière. Make what deductions you please for the vulgarity of the subjects—yet in the research, the profundity, the absolute truth and precision of the delineation of character,—in the invention of incident, in wit and humour, in life and motion, in everlasting variety and originality,—they never have been, and probably never will be, surpassed. They stimulate the faculties, as well as amuse them. As Charles Lamb has said, "Other pictures we see, Hogarth's we read!"

ARTS, supplement to the fourth, fifth and sixth editions (1816–24). By William Hazlitt (1778–1830), the writer and critic.

Hypatia

Hypatia is one of those whose names are glorified rather by wrongs than by merits; and had she not died, few would now know, and fewer care, whether she ever lived. [She was a teacher of Neoplatonic philosophy in Christian Alexandria and was cruelly murdered by a mob during a riot in A.D. 415.]

Her tragedy is well known by the account of Gibbon, drawn from *Socrates*, bk. vii., §15; and from Theodoret, who asserts Cyril's complicity. Theodoret knew Cyril [bishop of Alexandria] well enough to suspect him of anything; at least, to say of him, after his death, that "the only fear was that hell would find him too unpleasant a guest, and send him back to earth." And certainly all we know of him justifies the sneer; at least, it seems certain that Cyril protected her murderers.

Hypatia's death seems to have happened thus:— The minds of the Nitrian monks, and of the Alexandrian populace, had been inflamed by her intimacy with Orestes, the prefect, who was at open war with Cyril. Hating her both as what she was, the championess of an eclectic Polytheism; and as what she was not, a profligate woman, they laid wait for her at the door of that lecture-room in the Mouseion, where (to the envy of Cyril) her admirers' chariots and slaves were wont to wait. She was seized, stript naked, dragged into the Kaisareion (then a Christian church), and torn piece-meal, with fragments of shells and pottery. The flesh was scraped from the bones, and what remained burned in the Kinaron.

Thus ended, or seems to have ended, the last noble woman whom Greek paganism produced. But, indeed, Hypatia is at best but a myth and a shade; and two centuries more saw her transfigured into the famous Saint Catharine of Alexandria [an unproved theory]; the Christians whom she opposed into pagan philosophers confuted; Cyril into Maxentius the persecutor, the pot-sherds of the Kinaron into the toothed wheels miraculously broken by lightning from heaven; and Hypatia installed for a thousand years to come as one of the four virgin saints of Christendom. So does the whirligig of Time bring round its revenges; and every noble soul, even under a feigned name and circumstance, has its nobleness acknowledged, and does —not the work which it intended, but the work of which it was really capable.

HYPATIA, eighth edition (1853–60). By Charles Kingsley (1819–1875), clergyman, poet and novelist, author of the novel *Hypatia*, which, however, is not reliable as a historical source.

Death of Queen Elizabeth I

Elizabeth continued to reign with great glory till the year 1603; but all her greatness could not prevent her from being extremely miserable before her death. She had caused her greatest favourite, and probably her lover, the earl of Essex, to be executed. Though this execution could not be called unjust, the queen's affection (on being informed that he had at last thrown himself entirely on her clemency) returned to such a degree, that she thenceforth gave herself entirely over to despair. She refused food and sustenance; she continued silent and gloomy; sighs and groans were the only vent she gave to her despondence; and she lay for ten days and nights upon the carpet, leaning on cushions, which her maids brought her. Perhaps the faculties of her mind were impaired by long and violent exercise; perhaps she reflected with remorse on some past actions of her life, or perceived, but too strongly, the decays of nature, and the approach of her dissolution. She saw her courtiers remitting in their assiduity to her, in order to pay their court to James the apparent successor. Such a concurrence of causes was more than sufficient to destroy the remains of her constitution; and her end was now visibly seen to approach. Feeling a perpetual heat in her stomach, attended with an unquenchable thirst, she drank without ceasing, but refused the assistance of her physicians. Her distemper gaining ground, Cecil and the lord admiral desired to know her sentiments with regard to the succession. To this she replied, That as the crown of England had always been held by kings, it ought not to devolve upon any inferior character, but upon her immediate heir the king of Scotland. Being then advised by the archbishop of Canterbury to fix her thoughts upon God, she replied, that her thoughts did not in the least wander from him. Her voice soon after left her; she fell into a lethargic slumber, which continued some hours; and she expired gently without a groan, in the 70th year of her age, 45th of her reign.

ENGLAND, second edition (1777–83).

Opposition to the Act of Union, 1707, in Edinburgh

The tumults to which the city had been so frequently subject were revived in 1706, on the occasion of the proposed union of the kingdoms. This, as is well known, was at first an exceedingly unpopular measure in Scotland; and the consequence was a series of the most violent and outrageous proceedings on the part of the mob, in order to intimidate those members of the Scottish parliament who were favourable to the obnoxious project. The deed, however, was finally accomplished, though not without great danger to the lives of its most active promoters. A small summer house in the Regent Murray's garden is still pointed out as the place where the last signatures were attached to the document which terminated the independence of Scotland as a separate kingdom.

EDINBURGH, seventh edition (1830–42).

The Balance of Power in Europe

The states of Europe at present [c. 1815] are 57 in number and, considered with respect to political importance, may be divided into four classes. Britain, France, Russia, Austria, and Prussia, belong to the first; Spain, Sweden, Turkey, and the Netherlands, to the second; Portugal, Naples, Bavaria, Sardinia, Denmark, Saxony, Wirtemberg, Hanover, and Switzerland, to the third; Baden, Tuscany, and the States of the Church, with the other small states of Germany and Italy, belong to the fourth class. Objections may be made to this classification, but we have not been able to find a better; and a few remarks will explain the principle on which it is founded. The first five powers are the only powers that exercise a decided influence over their neighbours; and it is by their joint counsels that differences among the smaller powers are adjusted, and all questions that concern the general state of Europe decided. The four states of the second class visibly occupy a lower place in the scale of power than those of the first. They have very little exterior influence, but they are not directly controlled by any of the stronger powers; and it is only among them and the states of the first class that wars are now likely to originate. The third class includes those states which are too feeble, and too much under the influence of the great powers to become principals in war, but are of importance enough to be valued as auxiliaries by states of the first and second classes. The fourth class consists of states which have too little force to maintain any degree of independence, and owe their existence to the justice, the forbearance, or the mutual jealousies of the stronger powers. It is only in Europe that small states exist among large ones; and their existence is the consequence of that equality of power among the great states, which compels each to respect the rights of the others, and to pay a certain degree of deference to public opinion. The close union among four of the powers of the first rank since 1813, has established their influence over the rest of Europe much more firmly than at any former period.

EUROPE, supplement to the fourth, fifth and sixth editions (1816–24). By Charles Maclaren (1782–1866), the first editor of the *Scotsman* and a fellow of the Royal Society of Edinburgh.

Poverty in Ireland

The dress of the people is so wretched, that, to a person who has not visited the country, it is almost inconceivable. Shoes or stockings are seldom to be seen on children and often not on grown persons. The rags in which both men and women are clothed are so worn and complicated, that it is hardly possible to imagine to what article of dress they have originally belonged. It has been observed that the Irish poor never take off their clothes when they go to bed; but the fact is, that not only are they in general destitute of blankets, but, if they once took off their clothes, it would be difficult to get them on again. Their dress is worn day and night till it literally falls to pieces; and even when it is first put on, it is usually cast-off clothing; for there is not one cottager out of ten who ever gets a coat made for himself. A considerable trade has long been carried on from the west of Scotland to Ireland, consisting of the *old clothes* of the former country, and to those who know how long all ranks in Scotland wear their dress, there is no more convincing proof of the poverty of the latter country can be given.

IRELAND, supplement to the fourth, fifth and sixth editions (1816–24).

Albania

Albania, a province of Turkey in Europe, on the gulf of Venice, bounded by Livadia on the south, by Thessaly and Macedonia on the east, and on the north by Bosnia and Dalmatia. The people are strong, large, courageous, and good horsemen; but are said to be of a thievish disposition.

ALBANIA, fourth edition (1800–10).

The German People

The Germans in their persons are tall and strong built. The ladies have generally fine complexions; and some of them especially in Saxony, have all the delicacy of features and shape that are so bewitching in a certain island of Europe.

Both men and women affect rich dresses, which in fashion are the same as in France and England; but the better sort of men are excessively fond of gold and silver lace, especially if they are in the army. The ladies at the principal courts differ not much in their dress from the French and English, only they are not so excessively fond of paint as the former. At some

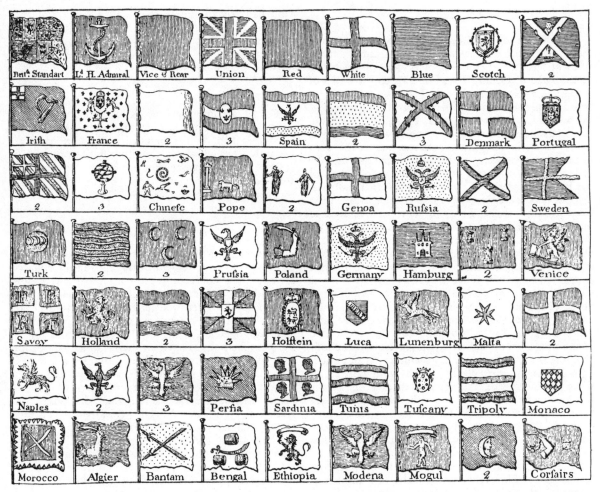

Flags of certain states, from the first edition (1768–71).

courts they appear in rich furs; and all of them are loaded with jewels, if they can obtain them. The female part of the burghers' families, in many German towns, dress in a very different manner, and some of them inconceivably fantastic. As to the peasantry and labourers, they dress as in other parts of Europe, according to their employments, conveniency, and opulence. In Westphalia, and most other parts of Germany, they sleep between two feather-beds, or rather the upper one of down, with sheets stitched to them, which by use becomes a very comfortable practice. The most unhappy part of the Germans are the tenants of little needy princes, who squeeze them to keep up their own grandeur; but, in general the circumstances of the common people are far preferable to those of the French.

The Germans are naturally a frank, honest, hospitable people, free from artifice and disguise. The higher orders are ridiculously proud of titles, ancestry, and show. The Germans, in general, are thought to want animation, as their persons promise more vigour and activity than they commonly exert even in the field of battle. But when commanded by able generals, especially the Italians, such as Montecuculi and prince Eugene they have done great things both against the Turks and the French.

Industry, application, and perseverance, are the great characteristics of the German nation, especially the mechanical parts of it. Their works of art would be incredible were they not visible, especially in watch and clock making, jewellery, turnery, sculpture, drawing, painting, and certain kinds of architecture. The Germans have been charged with intemperance in eating and drinking; and perhaps not unjustly, owing to the vast plenty of their country in wine and provisions of every kind. But those practices seem now to be wearing out. At the greatest tables, though the guests drink pretty freely during dinner, yet the repast is commonly finished by coffee after three or four public toasts have been drank. But no people have more feasting at marriages, funerals, and birthdays.

GERMANY, second edition (1777–83).

The Italians

In Italy the higher classes reside almost constantly in towns. During a few months in autumn, indeed some of them resort from Milan to villas on the banks of the Lake of Como; from Florence to the baths of Lucca; from Naples to Castello Mare, on the adjacent shores; and the Malaria of Rome drives the whole of the wealthier classes to Tivoli, Frescati, or Albano, during the dangerous season of August and September. Many villas, in beautiful situations, are to be seen round the Italian lakes, on the hills which surround the valley of the Arno, and on the enchanting shores of the Bay of Naples. But these are occasional, not permanent residences. Nowhere is a *country house*, in the English sense of the word, to be seen. The idea of building and living on his estate, seems never to enter the mind of an Italian proprietor. Field-sports are wholly unknown in the north of Italy, as might well be expected among a people whose habits are formed entirely to a city life. What they call going to shoot at Genoa, is sitting down in a little *bosco*, or wood, composed of ten or twelve young trees, in the corner of a garden, where the sportsman fires at crows and magpies, as they fly past. In Naples, however, the love of shooting is very common, and is particularly fashionable at Court; but the mode in which it is practised, by collecting an immense number of wild anmials, in some enclosed space, and firing at them as they issue from an outlet, accords but ill either with the feeling of *fair play* between the sportsman and his game which prevails in England, or with the active and energetic habits from which the love of it in this country has arisen. . . .

The universal disposition of the Italian proprietors to this mode of life, is the cause of the vast number of towns which are to be met with in every part of Italy, more especially in the plain of Lombardy; and of that polish of manners, which has descended so low in the scale of society. The coarseness which in this country too frequently disgraces the middling classes, and tarnishes the sterling virtues they possess, is there in a great degree unknown. The continual presence of all the higher orders, and the constant display of their manners in the places of general resort, has given to the middling and lower classes a degree of elegance, and a taste for the enjoyments of cultivated life, to which there is nothing comparable in any other part of Europe. Intoxication is almost entirely unknown, or, when it does occur, is looked upon with the utmost abhorrence. The amusements of the lower orders in the cities consist of dancing, singing, conversation, walking, and frequenting the public theatres. Even the peasants in the country participate in those elegant amusements, which seem natural to this genial climate. An English traveller benighted in the Appenines, near Carrara, two years ago (1819), not only met with a most hospitable reception from a small farmer, who refused to accept any remuneration, but was charmed the whole evening by his three daughters, who had recently completed their education at Leghorn, and sung in parts in the most beautiful manner. . . .

ITALY, supplement to the fourth, fifth and sixth editions (1816–24).

The Viennese

Of all accomplishments, a proficiency in music holds the highest place in the estimation of the Viennese; and, in the practice of this art, they are certainly as much above the other nations of Europe (except the Italians), as they are below them in more solid and useful pursuits.

VIENNA, eighth edition (1853–60).

The Russian Character

The accounts of the Russian character in the works of those who have resided or travelled in the country, are extremely conflicting. He who impartially weighs the evidence will arrive at the conclusion, which might have been suspected before the investigation began, that whilst there are not a few dark stains on the national character, many of them are attributable to the peculiar political system under which the people live, to their general ignorance hitherto, and to the low character and unclerical behaviour of the secular clergy; and that under a proper system of government, instruction, and religious discipline, the Russians would not be far behind some of their continental neighbours who hold a much higher place in the scale of civilization and morals. The opinion which generally prevails in this country regarding the Russians as a people does them injustice. If, as Dr Lyall asserts, they are "insinuating and cunning, deceitful and perfidious, sensual and immoral," it must not be forgotten, that any natural tendency to these vices not only remains unchecked by proper secular and religious instruction, but is fostered, as in a hotbed, by a state of slavery, or semi-vassalage, which is little better. Amongst all the nations of Europe, in Russia alone is one half of the population a marketable commodity, or something not very far removed from it. They are fond of novelties, amusements, and gambling, particularly of card-playing. They are extremely partial to singing, and their talents for imitation and the acquisition of languages are universally allowed to be remarkable. . . .

The national amusements are chiefly those afforded by the ice. A favourite diversion is the ice-hill, or mountain, as the Russians call it, on whose sides are formed steep inclined planes, down which the adventurer throws himself, seated on a machine, which he guides with surprising skill. Swinging is another Russian diversion; to which may be added the common ones of dancing, and of a national music, which, with the songs and ballads to which it is sung, is very plaintive and pleasing.

RUSSIA, seventh edition (1830–42). By John Francis Smith.

Whisky Smuggling in Scotland

Great pains have been taken to put an end to the practice of illicit distillation in Scotland; but hitherto this very desirable object has not been gained. The smugglers have set the whole force of government at defiance, and have carried on their processes in spite of all the attempts that have been made to stop them. Many of them, indeed, have been brought to absolute ruin, and few of them, we believe, have ever been able to realize much money or to rise to independence. But still a new race of smugglers has risen up after another to carry on their illicit trade, to the great detriment of the revenue, and to an equal deterioration of the morals of the common people. Government do not seem to have been aware of the principal reason of the continuance of this evil. They have bound down the legal distillers in such a manner by injurious restrictions, that it is not in their power to produce a spirit equal in flavour to that manufactured by the smugglers, who lie under none of those restrictions which bind down the ingenuity of the legal trader. This superiority induces a corresponding desire in the inhabitants of Scotland to possess themselves of smuggled whisky, even at a higher price than that for which they can purchase the same article from the licensed distillers. The smugglers, in consequence, are winked at, or rather encouraged, by a very considerable proportion of the inhabitants of the country. While this feeling exists, we may venture to predict, that it will be impossible to put an end to smuggling in Scotland.

DISTILLATION, supplement to the fourth, fifth and sixth editions (1816–24). By Thomas Thomson (1798–1869), historian and biographer.

British Judges in India

Among other causes of evils may be enumerated the incapacity of Europeans to officiate as judges in a society so peculiarly constituted as that of India, with the usages and manners of which, as well as with the general character of the people, they remain to this day in a great measure unacquainted. This is a fact which is deeply regretted by all the most experienced servants of the East India Company, from Sir John Shore downwards. Europeans are sent out to India with the sole view of amassing a fortune. They have no interest in the country from which they draw such important benefits. They know nothing of its habits and manners—never mixing with the natives in their ordinary business or amusements—and never attaining to more than a theoretical knowledge of their characters. With such qualifications, they begin to officiate as judges, how miserably ill-appointed for such an office their own experience quickly teaches them. They soon find the difficulty of appreciating or understanding even the most ordinary transactions of a society, with the rules and principles of which they are entirely unacquainted. What is intelligible by intuition to a native is a mystery to them; and it is easy to conceive how these difficulties must be accumulated on them in any long process of criminal judicature, involving a train of circumstantial, and frequently of contradictory evidence. It is not, as every one knows, on the mere naked testimony of a witness that a judge entirely relies; it is the tone, the manner, the living evidence of expression and character, which impresses upon testimony the stamp of truth; which carries conviction to the mind; and saves a judge from the miserable dilemma of being blown about by every wind of opposite evidence. These discriminations are, however, far too nice for a European judge in an Indian court, and he frequently knows not what to believe.

INDIA, supplement to the fourth, fifth and sixth editions (1816–24). By David Buchanan (1779–1848), journalist and author, editor of the *Edinburgh Courant.*

Africa: Trade, Colonization and Proposed Method of Civilization

With regard to the objects of trade in Africa, and particularly of export, these have presented a remarkable similarity, in all ages, and over every part of this continent. The first, and by far the most considerable, has always unhappily been the trade in the human species. Africa has in all ages been ransacked for those unfortunate beings, whose degradation was to be the instrument of pleasure or avarice to the lords of the other portions of the globe. Besides the European part of this atrocious traffic (ere long, it is to be hoped, to be fully, and for ever relinquished), there has long been a similar trade for the supply of Barbary and some countries of the East. The victims are drawn chiefly from the barbarous tribes inhabiting the central range of mountains. The whole number for this supply is estimated at twenty thousand. Part of these captives undergo a shameful mutilation, with a view of being placed in the seraglios of the East. In other respects, their lot is much milder than that of their West Indian brethren. They are used as domestics, are well treated, and often raised to posts of distinction.

Next to the human species, the article of exchange which Africa produces most abundantly, is gold.

IMPORTS (into Britain)

ARTICLES	1805 £	1810 £
Elephants' Teeth	10,285	16,488
Gum Arabic	3,947	8,420
— Senegal	16,223	46,384
Hides, raw and tanned	1,257	12,714
Skins and Furs	10,853	76,437
Wax, Bees	2,009	12,996
Red Wood	51,311	26,058
All other articles	10,960	57,790
Official value	106,845	257,387
Real Value	193,034	535,577

Map of Africa, from the first edition (1768–71).

EXPORTS (from Britain)

ARTICLES	1805 £	1810 £
Brass and Copper	12,085	3,231
Cotton Manufactures	285,408	196,214
Gunpowder	27,154	7,887
Guns	48,500	6,393
Iron and Steel	17,703	19,139
Woollens	78,394	68,402
India Piece Goods	324,087	59,967
Brandy and Geneva	8,490	1,722
Rum	56,181	7,551
All other articles	132,573	113,579
Official value	990,575	484,082
Real Value	1,156,985	693,911

On adverting to the future prospects of Africa, it is proper to say something, in the first place, as to the means of its more perfect exploration. It seems, then, to be now universally admitted, that no reliance can be placed on the common plan of solitary enterprize, or where the traveller has only one or two attendants. Nor is the device of assuming the character of a Mahometan likely to be repeated. Mahometanism is not a mere creed; it is a system, which regulates the whole train of thoughts and habits, and which moulds from infancy even the outward aspect and deportment. It is vain to expect, that the study of Arabic at an European seminary, or even a few months residence in the East, could mould all the habits of an European into a shape, which would enable him to deceive the watchful eyes of Musulmen. It appears also, that, while the character of a professed Christian is sufficiently detested, that of one who assumes a false semblance of Mahometanism is viewed with a much higher degree of reprobation. To the disguise, therefore, which Hornemann assumed, it is probable that this unfortunate traveller was partly indebted for his melancholy fate. The only mode, then, it would appear, of penetrating into Africa with any prospect of success, is to carry an armed force, which shall not be so large as to excite alarm, and yet sufficient to guard against desultory or sudden attack. Such an expedition would the less tend to excite jealousy, that Africa is habitually traversed by parties of this description for commercial purposes. . . .

The plan upon which the main reliance for the civilization of this region seems at present to be placed is, that of an extensive system of colonization. It is observed by Mr. Macaulay, Ex-secretary of the African Institution, that it is "necessary to the *rapid* growth of improvement, that men should be brought to live together in considerable bodies; that they should be protected by just laws; and that they should enjoy the means of instruction." This, he conceives, can only be effected in Africa by means of a colony, of some extent, composed of natives. The difficulty of collect-

ing a large native population is admitted, indeed, to be very great. The Africans, from many causes, and particularly from superstition, will not *voluntarily* resort to such a colony. A plan had, therefore, been suggested, in reference to the colony of Sierra Leone, to redeem the Grumettas, or native slaves, and transplant them to that establishment; but this plan was, after mature deliberation, and apparently upon very solid grounds, rejected. Even though some unexceptionable mode of collecting a mass of native population could be devised, we greatly suspect, that it would, in the end, be found still more difficult, if not impossible, to prevent those evils and abuses, which seem almost inseparable from the management of these distant establishments; and perhaps the friends of Africa would act more wisely, in limiting their views to coast settlements, solely for the purposes of opening and maintaining a ready communication with the natives. For our own parts, we are inclined to think, that if any thing farther ought to be attempted, the growth of civilization in Africa is more likely to be accelerated by calling to our aid the agency of their own chiefs, than by any attempts at extended colonization. We believe it to be conformable to the tenor of history, that some species of *compulsion* is necessary to the *speedy* civilization of barbarians; and that it is only in this way that their inveterate habits of sloth and indolence can be overcome. *Conquest*, therefore, has hitherto been the chief means of spreading civilization. The only kind of *compulsion* applicable with this view to Africa, is that which might be exercised by her native sovereigns. Our plan then would be, to invite some African chiefs to Europe, not to learn to read and write, but to show them the value of those branches of art, and means of opulence, the transplantation of which would render their own power more extensive, and more brilliant. Were an ambition of this kind once kindled in one or two active chiefs, *their* authority would soon, it is probable, effect a decisive change among their listless countrymen. But in order to give success to such a plan, all fear of conquest, or interference on our part, must be removed; and the ablest, most powerful and also the most *absolute* chiefs, must be courted and employed, as the properest instruments for effecting such a revolution.

AFRICA, supplement to the fourth, fifth and sixth editions (1816-24). By Hugh Murray (1779-1846), fellow of the Royal Society of Edinburgh and eminent geographer whose *magnum opus* was the *Encyclopaedia of Geography, a Description of the Earth, physical, statistical, civil and political* (published in London, 1834).

Humane Treatment of Negro Slaves in the U.S. Creates a Problem

It may be safely said, that the superior humanity of the Americans in the treatment of the blacks is the greatest obstacle to that abolition of slavery which they so ardently wish to accomplish, and that, were their slaves worked and fed like those in the West

Indies, the race of blacks, instead of multiplying ten-fold in the course of one century, would be entirely extinguished. The existence of slavery is a bequest from Britain; it is not the crime of the Americans, but their misfortune. It is an evil which they deplore, and of which they would gladly rid themselves if they knew how. The difficulty is, how to dispose of the slaves, whom many would be willing to manumit. The plan of carrying them back to a colony on the African coast seems absolutely chimerical; and the strong distinction of colour, with the rooted prejudices of the whites, form an insuperable bar to such an amalgamation of the two races as took place when the serfs of Western Europe were incorporated with the freemen in the fifteenth and sixteenth centuries.

UNITED STATES, supplement to the fourth, fifth and sixth editions (1816–24). By Charles Maclaren (1782–1866), the first editor of the *Scotsman* and a fellow of the Royal Society of Edinburgh.

United States of America

Such was the end of the contest between Great Britain and America: A contest in which the latter attained to an independent rank among the nations, that may be productive of more important consequences than can yet be foreseen; and in which the former, happily for herself, was forced to relinquish a sovereignty that served only to repress her own internal industry, and retard her prosperity. She has, in the event, only suffered a diminution of unwieldly empire which has been more than compensated by an increase of population, commerce, revenues, and wealth. . . .

The whole territory of the United States contains by computation a million of square miles, in which are 640 millions of acres. Of these, 51 millions are water; deducting which the total amount of acres of land in the United States is 589 millions.

That part of the United States comprehended between the west temporary line of Pensylvania on the east, the boundary line between Britain and the United States extending from the river St. Croix to the north-west extremity of the lake of the woods on the north, the river Missisippi to the mouth of the Ohio on the west, and the river Ohio on the south (the afore-mentioned bounds of Pensylvania), contains by computation about 411,000 square miles, in which are 26,340,000 acres. Deduct for water 4,340,000 acres; there remains 220 millions of acres.

The whole of this immense extent of unappropriated western territory, or vacant unsettled land, containing as above stated 220 millions of acres, has been by the cession of some of the original states, and by the treaty of peace, transferred to the fœderal government, and is pledged as a fund for sinking the continental debt. It is in contemplation to divide it into new states, with republican constitutions, similar to the old states near the Atlantic Ocean.

AMERICA, third edition (1788–97).

Colonization as a Furtherance of Trade and Wealth

There is no doubt that increasing and multiplying the British stock increases the producing and trading populations over the earth. Hence, if we can conveniently spare a portion of our people to inhabit distant regions, it may be politic to aid them by a government staff and other provisions in making a settlement. It happens that in general this country has not only been able to spare a portion of her citizens, but has found a relief in seeing them depart from her shores. To those indeed who have fallen into an unproductive and unhappy position in the mother country, the fresh emigration field has had the same effect as a supply of capital; for the occupation and use of a piece of productive land which has not previously been productively applied is to those who take it equivalent to the obtaining of so much capital. It is for the purpose of protecting if not creating emigration fields, that our colonial system has thus extended itself, and hence the more important considerations connected with it came under the head of Emigration. Wherever we can plant a numerous and prosperous body of the British people, we create a trading population which will increase our own commerce; and if it be said that they take capital out of the country to employ it elsewhere, after the secondary answer that colonists do not generally remove much capital, the main answer is, that for a nation like the British, in the full enjoyment of free trade, the best part of the world for their capital to be placed in, is that where it is most productive. Hence, the removal of a portion of our people, and with them of a portion of our capital, may tend to increase the trade and wealth of Britain. This phenomenon is at present very distinctly exemplified in our Australian colonies, and it is the principle on which, along with those of New Zealand and the additions to the North African colonies, they have been created and supported.

COLONY, eighth edition (1853–60). By John Hill Burton (1809–81), journalist and advocate, historiographer of Scotland.

Britain's Material Superiority to France

It is in vain, therefore, that France possesses a superior European population. In the state of things now described, it is impossible for her to support the same number of European soldiers that Britain may do. Every soldier France sends out must be maintained and clothed by the industry of Frenchmen, exerted upon a European soil, of far inferior fertility to that which is cherished by tropical rains, or the periodical floods of the Ganges. Whereas the British soldier is not supported merely by British industry, but by the industry of the natives of Hindostan, or of the labourers of Jamaica. In this view, by curtailing in a moderate degree her luxury, Britain might convert an immense proportion of her population to military service, so as far to exceed any numbers, that during a length of time, France could maintain in arms against her; for this simple reason, that almost every British subject may be said to be supported by the labour of eight or ten persons, in a more fertile country than that of France. In this respect, Britain resembles ancient Sparta. The citizens of that state were free, but each of them was a soldier, because he was supported by the industry of a subjugated race called *Helots*. What these last were to the Spartans, the Hindoos in the East, and the Africans transported to the West India islands, now are to the British nation.

It is also to be remarked, that the industry exerted in Britain is of a more profitable nature than that of France, in as much as manufacturing and commercial states always acquire greater riches than those employed in agriculture alone. We are, therefore, better able to support the expence of a protracted war, than the French can possibly be. Nor is any injury which they can do to our commerce an object of serious alarm. By refusing to trade with us, they only prevent themselves from acquiring wealth. All Asia and America are open to us, and no exertions of political power have hitherto been found able to exclude the British manufactures from the continent of Europe.

Even the engines of war, we possess in a superior degree to France. In consequence of the expertness of our artists, all kinds of instruments of destruction are here produced in greater abundance and with more facility; and our wealth has given us the command of the means of bringing into the field an innumerable cavalry, which could not fail instantly to embarrass an invading enemy, and by cutting off every means of communication or supply, ultimately to reduce them to ruin, with little loss or difficulty to ourselves. We are, indeed, accustomed greatly to overrate the evils attending invasion.

BRITAIN, fourth edition (1800–10).

Labour Unrest, 1830

Even England began to rival Ireland in misery and disturbances. While parliament continued to sit, its table was covered with petitions, describing in the strongest terms the distress suffered by the lower classes engaged in agriculture. It was predicted that unless a change for the better took place it would be impossible to restrain them from outrage. The harvest was scarcely concluded when this prophecy was fulfilled. The disturbances began in the county of Kent. Threatening letters were dispersed throughout the county, machinery destroyed, money extorted, and barns and stack-yards set on fire. The commotions were the wild aimless efforts of men suffering almost beyond nature and without hope. Viewing the matter in this light, the first rioters apprehended were treated with a degree of lenity which encouraged fresh outrages. During October, November and December 1830, the riots increased in frequency and boldness,

and spread from Kent into Hants, Wilts, Bucks, Sussex, and Surrey. The frame of civil society seemed breaking up, and a wild deluge of human passion, untamed by moral feeling, unchecked by law, threatened to overwhelm all.

With a nation apparently resolving into anarchy, and a government helpless and stubborn, there was no hope. Like sailors in a shipwreck, men began to search for something to cling to in the impending convulsion. The demand for reform was raised more clamorously than ever. Political unions and reform associations, having for their object the propagation of definite political principles, and a demonstration of the physical strength of the reformers, were everywhere established. The most important of these bodies were the Birmingham union, the model of all the others; the great northern union, extending over Northumberland and Durham; and the Renfrewshire political union. But others of less note were to be found in almost every town and village in the kingdom.

Such was the threatening aspect of the country when parliament opened on the 2nd of November.

BRITAIN, seventh edition (1830–42).

Luxury Production the Sign of a Developed Economy

It was long a prevalent opinion among moralists, that the labour bestowed on the production of luxuries, and consequently their consumption, was unproductive. But this opinion is now almost universally abandoned. Unless, indeed, all comforts and enjoyments are to be proscribed, it is impossible to say where necessaries end, and luxuries begin. But if we are to understand by necessaries such products only as are absolutely required for the support of human life, every thing but wild fruits, roots, and water, must be deemed superfluous; and in this view of the matter, the peasantry of Ireland, who live only on potatoes and butter-milk, must be considered as contributing much more to the national wealth than the peasantry of Britain! The mere statement of such a doctrine is sufficient for its refutation. Every thing that stimulates exertion is advantageous. The mere necessaries of life may be detained with comparatively little labour; and those savage and uncivilized hordes, who have no desire to possess its comforts, are proverbially and notoriously indolent and dissipated. To make men industrious—to make them shake off that lethargy which is natural to them, they must be inspired with a taste for the luxuries and enjoyments of civilized life When this is done, their artificial wants will become equally clamorous with those that are strictly necessary, and they will increase exactly as the means of gratifying them increase. Whenever a taste for comforts and conveniences has been generally diffused, the wants and desires of man become altogether unlimited. The gratification of one leads directly to the formation of another. In highly civilized societies, new products and new modes of enjoyment are constantly presenting themselves as motives to exertion, and as means of rewarding it. Perseverance is, in consequence, given to all the operations of industry; and idleness, and its attendant train of evils, almost entirely disappear.

POLITICAL ECONOMY, supplement to the fourth, fifth and sixth editions (1816–24). By J. R. McCulloch (1789–1864), statistician and economist, and the first professor of political economy at London university.

Consequences of the Poor-Law System

The practical operation of the poor-law system [the "Speenhamland System"] is as follows: Every labourer is presumed to require a gallon loaf of standard wheaten bread, weekly, for every member of his family, and one over: *i.e.* four loaves for three persons: seven for six.—A.B. has a wife and four children; he claims seven gallon loaves, costing, we will suppose, 12s. But his wages are only 9s.: therefore the parish supplies him with 3s. weekly. C.D. has a wife and six children; he requires nine gallon loaves, or 14s. 8d. He earns 10s.; the parish makes up the rest. E.F. is so idle and disorderly, that no one will employ him: but he has a wife and five children, and requires eight gallon loaves for their support. His allowance, then, is 9s. in lieu of the wages which he ought to earn, and 5s. or 6s. to make up the deficiency of these wages. . . .

Every new experiment in legislation is interesting to the philosophical inquirer, and valuable to the practical statesman. A system like that which we have been describing, in particular, has placed the inhabitants of a great country in so new and untried a predicament, that it becomes a matter of singular importance, to trace its effects, political and moral. The poor, it must be acknowledged, in all crowded and highly civilized states, present a problem of great embarrassment. Where so much wealth and so much penury are seen in opposition; where there is on the one side so much superfluity, on the other so much deficiency; a plan which promises a nearer equalization of the comforts of life brings a strong recommendation, at first sight, to the best feelings of the legislator and the moralist. On this account, our English system of poor-laws has been the subject of frequent eulogy;—has been glanced at with a view to its adoption both with reference to France and Ireland; though the rulers of these countries have hitherto been wisely contented rather to take our warning than to follow our example. Scotland is still in a more hesitating state.

1. The first, and perhaps the greatest of the political mischiefs occasioned by the poor-laws is this; that they disturb the due proportion between the supply of labourers and the demand for labour. They encourage population, without reference to the funds by which that population is to be supported. They persuade the lower classes to marry as soon as inclination prompts, as if it were needless to reflect whether they can maintain the probable issue of that marriage. . . .

This leads us on to the second mischief arising out of the present state of the poor-laws, which is closely connected with the preceding. They tend to overburthen the land, upon which the funds for their support are charged; and thus to introduce a system of universal pauperism. . . .

Already has the claim, in very many instances, exceeded the available resources. In numerous and extensive districts, during the years 1816, 1817, and 1818, it proved impossible for the contributor to furnish the quota which the necessities of those without labour, and, therefore, without support, demanded. Admission into the work and alms-houses, once dreaded as the last resort of hopeless penury, has been courted as a boon, and accepted as a favour. Whilst in London, and other great towns, many almost starving families were deterred from applying to the parish by the crowded, unhealthy, and horrible state of the workhouses into which they would be received, if indeed they could be received at all; many parishes were absolutely unable to raise the assessments, the increase of which, according to the existing laws, has tended only to bring more and more persons upon the parish, and to make what was collected less and less effectual; and yet there was an almost universal cry from one end of the kingdom to the other for voluntary charity to come in aid of the parochial assessments. . . .

Now it will appear, that as the price of corn in 1815 and in 1820 was the same, the amount of the rates ought likewise to have been the same, with the addition of ten *per cent.* for increase of population. It ought, therefore, to have been six million pounds in 1820, according to the scale of 1815 [about five-and-a-half million pounds]. But it is *seven* million pounds, giving a million, or one-sixth of the whole, as the actual growth of five years. This surely must satisfy every doubt concerning the ruinous tendency of the system, and shows that the only remaining question must be, not whether the evil is in its own nature progressive, but how progressive evil may be most wisely and effectually restrained. . . .

2. Another injurious effect of the poor-laws is the bad and discontented temper which is generated by ignorance of the real causes of poverty. Almost every thing which has hitherto been done for the poor has tended, as if with care and intention, to throw a veil of obscurity over this subject, and to hide from them the real origin of their difficulties. In all cases, the last man whom any one, labouring under misfortune, is *inclined* to accuse, is himself. But the poor-system tends to maintain the opinion, that he is the last person who *ought* to be accused. The workman who can find no employment; the labourer who feels his large and increasing family a burthen which he can ill support; the aged and decrepit, whose pittance barely furnishes

them with the necessaries of life; each lay the fault of their particular distress upon the parish, or upon the overseer, or upon the magistrate: but never blame their own imprudence in neglecting a provision, or their extravagance in throwing one away. And when relieved, to the full extent that legal charity can relieve them, they never acknowledge any sense of obligation. . . .

"I cannot help believing," says Malthus, "that, if the poor in this country were convinced, that they had no claim of *right* to support, and yet in scarcities, and all cases of urgent distress, were liberally relieved, which I think they would be, the bonds which unite the rich with the poor would be drawn much closer than at present; and the lower classes of society, as they would have less real reason for irritation and discontent, would be much less subject to such uneasy sensations."

3. To this habitual discontent is to be added the selfishness and mercenary spirit arising from the habit of looking to parochial assistance in every emergency. . . .

There are other immoral consequences of the poor-laws which are too obvious to need particular illustration. Husbands are encouraged to desert their wives, and fly from the burthen of their families, knowing that they will not be unprovided for. Women are encouraged to admit illicit intercourse, from a confidence that if it should prove fruitful, a marriage will be probably forced from the ordinary operation of the laws; a calculation which begins in vice, and can only end in premature and ill-sorted marriages.

POOR-LAWS, supplement to the fourth, fifth and sixth editions (1816–24). By John Bird Sumner (1780–1862), who afterward became archbishop of Canterbury.

The above was written during a period of very high poor-law expenditure, amounting to a fifth of all public expenditure, and of some abuse of the system. It was reformed by the Poor Law Amendment act, 1834. The interested reader is directed to the treatment of the subject in the 1963 printing of the *Encyclopaedia Britannica* in the article POOR LAW, by Dorothy Marshall and Professor Asa Briggs.

Combination by Work-People

Combinations to raise wages or limit the hours of labour are [in the 1850s] perfectly legal, if they be unaccompanied by threats or violence. These measures have not, however, had all the effect which many of their supporters anticipated. And it must be admitted that the workmen have in many instances discovered a refractory and turbulent disposition, and that there is hardly a branch of industry in which they have not resorted to *strikes*, and entered into combinations to raise wages, and to dictate to their masters the mode in which they should be employed. But though much to be regretted, this, after all, is only what might have been fairly expected. Great stress had long been laid, in the public estimation, on the efficacy of the combination laws. The workmen had been punished for entering into combinations, because it was supposed

that they might thereby force up wages to an undue elevation; and when such notions, though false and unfounded, were embodied in the statute book and proclaimed from the bench, it need not excite surprise that they were credited by the work-people. Nothing, indeed, could be more natural than that the latter, when they were emancipated from the restraints of the law, should endeavour to avail themselves of what was supposed to be the powerful resource of combination. It should also be borne in mind that a large number of individuals began immediately to perceive that, whatever might be their influence in other respects, combinations might be turned to good account by those by whom they were organized and managed. But apart from the peculiar interests of such parties, it was but reasonable to suppose that for a while at least combinations would be in high favour with the working-classes; and that nothing but experience would suffice to convince them of their generally ruinous tendency. . . .

Nothing can apparently be more reasonable than that workmen should be allowed freely to combine or associate together, for the purpose of adjusting the terms on which they will sell their labour. Wages, like every thing else, should always be left to be regulated by the fair and free competition of the parties in the market, without being interfered with by the legislature. But workmen are not allowed freely to dispose of their labour, if they be prevented from concerting with each other the terms on which they will sell it. Capacity to labour is to the poor what stock is to the capitalists. Now a hundred or a thousand capitalists may form themselves into a company, or combination, take all their measures in common, and dispose of their property as they may, in their collective capacity, judge most advantageous for their interests:—And why should not a hundred or a thousand labourers be allowed to do the same by their stock? Of all the varieties of property which a man can possess, the faculties of his mind and the powers of his body are most particularly his own. And to fetter him in the mode in which he is to exercise or dispose of these faculties and powers, is a manifest encroachment on the most inviolable of all rights, and can be justified only by an overwhelming necessity. . . .

But notwithstanding the dear-bought experience of their generally injurious influence, strikes and combinations to raise wages have seldom been so prevalent as in the past year, 1853. They seem to have originated in a variety of circumstances; partly and principally, perhaps, in the diminution of the supply of labour, occasioned by the extraordinary emigration to Australia and the United States, and partly in the increase of the exports, and the exaggerated statements put forth in relation to the profits of the manufacturers. . . .

The work-people should also bear in mind, when they engage in strikes and combinations to force up wages, that capital is not bound to any peculiar locality. Manufactures have been driven, in more than one instance, from one part of this country to another, through the disorderly and turbulent conduct of the work-people. But the mischief may go farther than this. Strikes and combinations, on a great scale, like those at present (March 1854) existing, may force capital to another country. . . .

It must not be imagined that this is the only country in which manufacturing industry may be successfully prosecuted. Many parts of Prussia, Saxony, Switzerland, and France, have extensive and flourishing manufactures. And we do not know anything half so likely to stimulate their industry, and to make their competition still more dangerous than at present, as the strikes and combinations so frequent in England. They not only paralyze the proceedings of our manufacturers, but they tempt them to become partners in foreign houses, to construct mills on the Rhine or the Seine, rather than on the Irwell or the Clyde, and to carry abroad their machinery and their best workmen. And we are sorry to have to say that these are not speculative or eventual circumstances. They are being realized at this very moment (1853–54). . . .

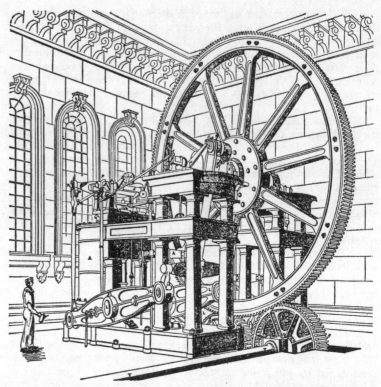

Steam engine, from the seventh edition (1830–42).

These remarks proceed from no unfriendly feeling towards the workmen, but from a desire to do them service. It is the extreme of folly to suppose that any combination can maintain wages at an artificial elevation. It is not on the dangerous and generally ruinous resource of combination, but on the forethought, industry, and frugality of work-people, that their wages, and their condition as individuals, must always depend.

COMBINATION, eighth edition (1853–60). By J. R. McCulloch (1789–1864), statistician and economist, and the first professor of political economy at London university. [This article was written after 1825—when trade unions were given a legal right to exist but were severely restricted in their actions—and before the Trade Union act of 1871 assured them of legal status. The 1963 printing of the *Encyclopaedia Britannica* in the article INDUSTRIAL RELATIONS puts it thus: "Until 1824 trade unions were illegal in Great Britain, and for the next half century they were handicapped by many legal restrictions, such as the laws on conspiracy and the common-law principle by which action in restraint of trade was illegal. Not only were trade unions hampered by such laws and by the hostility of the courts, but they encountered bitter opposition from employers . . ."]

Replacement of Spinners by Machinery in the Cotton Industry

In the present century a machine has been constructed which promises almost to out-vie all others in importance; it is the self-acting mule, the invention of Messrs Sharp, Roberts, and Company of Manchester. The last patent was taken out in 1830; and there are now nearly half a million of spindles at work on the principle of spinning yarn almost independently of human labour.

The history of this invention is fraught with instruction to the working classes. Attention was first directed to the possibility of contriving a self-acting mule, in consequence of the frequency of "turns-out" amongst the spinners, and the intolerable domination which they were enabled to exercise, from the circumstance of a comparatively small class of workmen having it in their power at any moment to suspend the whole trade of cotton spinning. One "spinner" has three or four young hands immediately dependent upon himself; he has also four or five virtually dependent on him, inasmuch as they being occupied in preparing the raw cotton for him to spin, if he take a fit of idleness or insubordination, the preliminary processes are of course suspended. In the same way, if the spinners, as a body, become idle, the weavers, and eventually the bleachers, spinners, and printers, are brought to a stand; in fact, the whole cotton trade is locked up, and misery and privation are the immediate and widespread results. These considerations induced the master spinners, about ten years ago, to call into play the talent of ingenious men, for the purpose of constructing such a machine as would give more stability and regularity to the processes of spinning. This machine has the virtue of being easily grafted on the older-fashioned mules, a fifth of the value of which is sacrificed in making them self-acting.

MANCHESTER, seventh edition (1830–42).

Taxation of Income Impracticable

The difficulties in the way of assessing income are of two sorts: 1st, The difficulty of ascertaining the amount of the annual revenue of different individuals; and, 2nd, Supposing that amount to be known, the difficulty of laying an equal tax on incomes derived from different sources.

It would be useless to dwell at any considerable length on the first of these heads. Incomes arising from the rent of land and houses, mortgages, funded property, and such like sources, may be learned with tolerable precision; but it neither has been, and, we are bold to say, never will be, possible to determine the incomes of farmers, manufacturers, dealers of all sorts, and professional men, with any thing like even the rudest approximation to accuracy. It is in vain to attempt to overcome this insuperable difficulty by instituting an odious inquiry into the affairs of individuals. It is not, indeed, very likely that any people, not altogether enslaved, would tolerate, in ordinary circumstances, such inquisitorial proceedings; but whether they did or did not, the result would be the same. The investigations would be worthless; and the commissioners of an income-tax would in the end have nothing to trust to but the declarations of the parties. Hence it is that the tax would fall with its full weight upon men of integrity, while the *millionaire* of "easy virtue" would well nigh escape it altogether. It would, in fact, be a tax on honesty, and a bounty on perjury and fraud; and, if carried to any considerable height—to such a height as to render it a prominent source of income—it would undoubtedly generate the most barefaced prostitution of principle, and would do much to obliterate that nice sense of honour which is the only sure foundation of national probity and virtue.

TAXATION, seventh edition (1830–42). By J. R. McCulloch (1789–1864), statistician and economist, and the first professor of political economy at London university.

The Middle Class

It is to be observed, that the class which is universally described as both the most wise and the most virtuous part of the community, the middle rank, are wholly included in that part of the community which is not the aristocratical. It is also not disputed, that in Great Britain the middle rank are numerous, and form a large proportion of the whole body of the people. The opinions of that class of the people who are below middle rank, are formed, and their minds are directed, by that intelligent and virtuous rank who come the most immediately in contact with them, who are in the constant habit of intimate communication with them, to whom they fly for advice and assistance in all their numerous difficulties, upon whom they feel an immediate and daily dependence, in health and in sickness, in infancy and in old age; to whom their children look up as models for their imitation, whose opinions they hear daily repeated, and account it their honour to adopt. There can be no doubt that the middle rank, which gives to science, to art, and to legislation itself, their most distinguished ornaments, the chief source of all that has exalted and refined human nature, is that portion of the community of which, if the basis of representation were ever so far extended, the opinion would ultimately decide. Of the people beneath them, a vast majority would be sure to be guided by their advice and example.

The incidents which have been urged as exceptions to this general rule, and even as reasons for rejecting it, may be considered as contributing to its proof. What signify the irregularities of a mob, more than half composed, in the greater number of instances, of boys and women, and disturbing, for a few hours or days, a particular town? What signifies the occasional turbulence of a manufacturing district, peculiarly unhappy from a very great deficiency of a middle rank, as there the population almost wholly consists of rich manufacturers and poor workmen; with whose minds no pains are taken by anybody; with whose afflictions there is no virtuous family in the middle rank to sympathize; whose children have no good example of such a family to see and to admire; and who are placed in the highly unfavourable situation of fluctuating between very high wages in one year, and very low wages in another? It is altogether futile, with regard to the foundation of good government, to say that this or the other portion of the people may at this or the other time depart from the wisdom of the middle rank. It is enough that the great majority of the people never cease to be guided by that rank; and we may, with some confidence, challenge the adversaries of the people to produce a single instance to the contrary in the history of the world.

GOVERNMENT, supplement to the fourth, fifth and sixth editions (1816–24). By James Mill (1773–1836), historian, economist and philosopher, and father of John Stuart Mill.

Chivalry

From these circumstances, the total decay of chivalrous principle is sufficiently evident. As the progress of knowledge advanced, men learned to despise its fantastic refinements; the really enlightened, as belonging to a system inapplicable to the modern state of the world; the licentious, fierce, and subtile, as throwing the barriers of affected punctilio, betwixt them and the safe, ready, and unceremonious gratification of their lust or their vengeance.

The system, as we have seen, had its peculiar advantages during the middle ages. Its duties were not, and indeed could not always be performed in perfection, but they had a strong influence on public opinion;

and we cannot doubt that its institutions, virtuous as they were in principle, and honourable and generous in their ends, must have done much good and prevented much evil. We can now only look back on it as a beautiful and fantastic piece of frostwork, which has dissolved in the beams of the sun! But though we look in vain for the pillars, the vaults, the cornices, and the fretted ornaments of the transitory fabric, we cannot but be sensible that its dissolution has left on the soil valuable tokens of its former existence. . . . Its effects are to be sought in the general feeling of respect to the female sex; in the rules of forbearance and decorum in society; in the duties of speaking truth and observing courtesy; and in the general conviction and assurance, that, as no man can encroach upon the property of another without accounting to the laws, so none can infringe on his personal honour, be the difference of rank what it may, without subjecting himself to personal responsibility.

CHIVALRY, supplement to the fourth, fifth and sixth editions (1816–24). By Sir Walter Scott (1771–1832).

Love

Every one is conscious of a pleasing emotion when contemplating beauty either in man or woman; and when that pleasure is combined with the gratification of the sensual appetite, it is obvious that the sum of enjoyment must be greatly increased. The perception of beauty, therefore, necessarily directs the energy of the sensual appetite to a particular object; but still this combination is a mere selfish feeling, which regards its object only as the best of many similar instruments of pleasure. Before it can deserve the name of love, it must be combined with esteem, which is never bestowed but upon moral character and internal worth; for let a woman be ever so beautiful, and of course ever so desirable as an instrument of sensual gratification, if she be not possessed of the virtues and dispositions which are peculiar to her sex, she will inspire no man with a generous affection. With regard to the outlines, indeed, whether of internal disposition or of external form, men and women are the same; but nature, intending them for mates, has given them dispositions which, though concordant, are however different, so as to produce together delicious harmony. The man more robust, is fitted for severe labour, and for field exercise; the woman, more delicate, is fitted for sedentary occupations, and particularly for nursing children. The man, bold and vigorous, is qualified for being a protector; the woman, delicate, and timid, requires protection. Hence it is that a man never admires a woman for possessing bodily strength or personal courage; and women always despise men who are totally destitute of these qualities. The man, as a protector, is directed by nature to govern; the woman, conscious of inferiority, is disposed to obey. Their intellectual powers correspond to the destination of nature. Men have penetration and solid judgment to

fit them for governing, women have sufficient understanding to make a decent figure under a good government; a greater portion would excite dangerous rivalship between the sexes, which nature has avoided by giving them different talents. Women have more imagination and sensibility than men, which make all their enjoyments more exquisite; at the same time that they are better qualified to communicate enjoyment. Add another capital difference of disposition: The gentle and insinuating manners of the female sex tend to soften the roughness of the other sex; and wherever women are indulged with any freedom, they polish sooner than men.

These are not the only particulars that distinguish the sexes. With respect to the ultimate end of love, it is the privilege of the male, as superior and protector, to make a choice; the female preferred has no privilege but barely to consent or to refuse. Whether this distinction be the immediate result of the originally different dispositions of the sexes, or only the effect of associations inevitably formed, may be questioned; but among all nations it is the practice for men to court, and for women to be courted; and were the most beautiful woman on earth to invert this practice, she would forfeit the esteem, however by her external grace she might excite the desire, of the man whom she addressed. The great moral virtues which may be comprehended under the general term integrity are all absolutely necessary to make either men or women estimable; but to procure esteem to the female character, the modesty peculiar to their sex is a very essential circumstance. Nature hath provided them with it as a defence against the artful solicitations of the other sex before marriage, and also as a support of conjugal fidelity.

LOVE, fourth edition (1800–10).

The Growth of Population and Its Checks

If, setting out from a tolerably well peopled country such as England, France, Italy, or Germany, we were to suppose that, by great attention to agriculture, its produce could be permanently increased every twenty-five years by a quantity equal to that which it at present produces, it would be allowing a rate of increase decidedly beyond any probability of realization. Yet this would be an arithmetical progression, and would fall short, beyond all comparison, of the natural increase of population in a geometrical progression, according to which the inhabitants of any country in 500 years, instead of increasing to twenty times, would increase to above a million times their present numbers.

It will be said, perhaps, that many parts of the earth are as yet very thinly peopled, and, under proper management, would allow of a much more rapid increase of food than would be possible in the more fully inhabited states of Europe. This is unquestionably true. Some parts of the earth would no doubt be capable of producing food at such a rate as to keep pace for a few periods with an unrestricted increase of population. But, to put this capacity fully into action, is of all things the most difficult.

But, supposing for a moment that the object could be fully accomplished, that is, supposing that the capacity of the earth to produce the necessaries of life could be put fully into action, and that they were distributed in the proportions most favourable for the growth of capital, and the effective demand for labour, the increase of population, whether arising from the increase of the inhabitants of each country, or from emigrants issuing from all those countries which were more advanced in cultivation, would be so rapid, that, in a period comparatively quite short, all the good lands would be occupied, and the rate of the possible increase of food would be reduced much below the arithmetical ratio above supposed.

But, if the natural increase of population, when unchecked by the difficulty of procuring the means of subsistence, or other peculiar causes, be such as to continue doubling its numbers in twenty-five years; and the greatest increase of food, which, for a continuance, could possibly take place on a limited territory like our earth in its present state, be at the most only such as would add every twenty-five years an amount equal to its present produce; it is quite clear that a powerful check on the increase of population must be almost constantly in action.

The great question, then, which remains to be considered, is the manner in which this constant and necessary check upon population practically operates. . . .

Though man has but a trifling and temporary influence in altering the proportionate amount of the checks to population, or the degree in which they press upon the actual numbers, yet he has a great and most extensive influence on their character and mode of operation. . . . The nature of those checks can be classed under the general heads of Preventive and Positive. . . . It will be found, that they are resolvable into *moral restraint, vice, and misery*. . . .

Moral restraint, in application to the present subject, may be defined to be, abstinence from marriage, either for a time or permanently, from prudential considerations, with a strictly moral conduct towards the sex in the interval. And this is the only mode of keeping population on a level with the means of subsistence, which is perfectly consistent with virtue and happiness. All other checks, whether of the preventive or the positive kind, though they may greatly vary in degree, resolve themselves into some form of vice or misery.

The remaining checks of the preventive kind, are the sort of intercourse which renders some of the women of large towns unprolific; a general corruption of morals with regard to the sex, which has a similar effect; unnatural passions and improper arts to prevent the consequences of irregular connections. These evidently come under the head of vice.

The positive checks to population include all the causes, which tend in any way prematurely to shorten the duration of human life; such as unwholesome occupations—severe labour and exposure to the seasons—bad and insufficient food and clothing arising from poverty—bad nursing of children—excesses of all kinds—great towns and manufactories—the whole train of common diseases and epidemics—wars, infanticide, plague, and famine. Of these positive checks, those which appear to arise from the laws of nature, may be called exclusively misery; and those which we bring upon ourselves, such as wars, excesses of all kinds, and many others, which it would be in our power to avoid, are of a mixed nature. They are brought upon us by vice, and their consequences are misery.

POPULATION, supplement to the fourth, fifth and sixth editions (1816–24). By Thomas Robert Malthus (1766–1834), the economist, whose classic work, *An Essay on the Principle of Population*, was first published in 1798. It is worth noting that the F.A.O. *Third World Survey* (1963) views the population/food ratio for the world today and some years to come just as gravely.

The London Press

The history of newspapers during the long reign of George III is a history of criminal prosecutions, in which individual writers and editors were repeatedly defeated and severely punished; whilst the press itself derived new strength from the protracted conflict, and turned ignominious penalties into signal triumphs. From the days of John Wilkes to those of Leigh Hunt, every conspicuous newspaper prosecution gave tenfold currency to the doctrines that were assailed; and if some timid malcontents were occasionally cowed into silence and retreat, the ranks were the stronger for their absence. In the earlier part of this period, men who were mere traders in politics—whose motives were obviously base, and their lives contemptible—became powers in the state, able to brave king, legislature, and law courts, by virtue of the simple truth that a free people must have a free press. Yet the policy that had utterly failed in 1763 continued to be clung to in 1819. . . .

The London weekly press has always worn a motley garb. In its ranks are to be found some of the most worthless newspapers and some of the best. Weekly publication facilitates the individuality of a journal, both as respects its editorship, and as respects the class of readers to which it more especially addresses itself. From the days of Daniel Defoe to those of Albany Fonblanque and Robert Rintoul, there have always been newspapers bearing the unmistakeable impress of an individual mind. And this characteristic quality, whilst it has strengthened and deepened the influence of good journals, has also, of necessity, increased the temporary power of bad journals. When to great force of character in the writer and its natural result, an almost personal intimacy between writer and reader, governments have been unwise enough to add the strength which inevitably grows out of persecution, the combination might well prove a formidable one. Cobbett's *Weekly Register* affords perhaps as striking an illustration of journalism, in its greatness and in its meanness, as could be culled from its entire annals since a newspaper was first issued.

NEWSPAPERS, eighth edition (1853–60). By Edward Edwards (1812–86), the distinguished librarian and library historian, who assisted Sir Anthony Panizzi in establishing the catalogue of the British Museum library. [This article, and that on the LIBERTY OF THE PRESS, an extract from which follows immediately, reflect the currents of opinion regarding the press and its liberty in the late 18th and early 19th centuries. Following the long fights of John Wilkes, the great champion of the freedom of the press, the right to publish parliamentary reports was granted in 1772. A stamp tax had been introduced on newspapers in 1712; it was abolished gradually after 1836, following the appearance, between 1831–35, of hundreds of unstamped newspapers with a fiercely revolutionary political tone. After its total abolition in 1861, the consequent drop in newspaper prices and the cheap postal service from 1840, the numbers and circulation of newspapers increased greatly.]

Liberty of the Press

There is scarcely a right, for the violation of which, scarcely an operation of government, for the disturbance of which the press may not be employed as an instrument. The offences capable of being committed by the press are indeed nearly co-extensive with the whole field of delinquency. . . .

So true it is that the discontent of the people is the only means of removing the defects of vicious governments, that the freedom of the press, the main instrument of creating discontent, is, in all civilized countries, among all but the advocates of misgovernment, regarded as an indispensable security, and the greatest safeguard of the interests of mankind. . . .

There can be no adequate check without the freedom of the press. The evidence of this is irresistible. In all countries, the people either have a power legally and peaceably of removing their governors, or they have not that power. If they have not that power, they can only obtain very considerable ameliorations of their governments by resistance, by applying physical force to their rulers, or, at least, by threats so likely to be followed by performance, as may frighten their rulers into compliance. But resistance, to have this effect, must be general. To be general, it must spring from a general conformity of opinion, and a general knowledge of that conformity. How is this effect to be produced, but by some means, fully enjoyed by the people, of communicating their sentiments to one another? Unless where the people can all meet in general assembly, there is no other means known to the world of attaining this object to be compared with the freedom of the press. . . .

We have then arrived at the following important conclusions,—that there is no safety to the people in allowing any body to choose opinions for them; that there are no marks by which it can be decided beforehand, what opinions are true and what are false; that there must, therefore, be equal freedom of declaring all opinions, both true and false; and that, when all opinions, true and false, are equally declared, the assent of the greater number, when their interests are not opposed to them, may always be expected to be given to the true. These principles, the foundation of which appears to be impregnable, suffice for the speedy determination of every practical question. . . .

LIBERTY OF THE PRESS, supplement to the fourth, fifth and sixth editions (1816–24). By James Mill (1773–1836), historian, economist and philosopher, and father of John Stuart Mill. [*See* also the note that follows the extract *The London Press* immediately above.]

Newspaper Reporting

Perhaps the most extraordinary part of the machinery of a morning paper is the reporting. The establishment of reporters varies, as already stated, from ten to fourteen; and most of the persons so engaged are gentlemen of education, sometimes students of law, remarkable for their activity and intelligence. During the session of parliament, the reporters of the leading papers attend by turns each day, from the time the business commences, one succeeding the other, according to previous arrangement, and each remaining in the house for half or three quarters of an hour. If the debate be not protracted, or "heavy," as it is called, the reporter in the House of Commons, when relieved, enters a small apartment at the end of the lobby, appropriated exclusively for the purpose, and there arranges his notes, which are seldom taken in short-hand, from the impossibility, in ordinary cases, of finding room in a newspaper for all that a member may say, or even the half of it. He then proceeds at once to the office of the paper on which he is engaged, and by him the attention of the editor is directed to any thing of commanding interest which may have transpired. His slips, as they are written, are handed by the printer to the compositors, whose number during the session of parliament is generally increased; and as one reporter follows another, it is not unusual for a debate which has terminated at midnight to be set up in types, and ready for printing, by two o'clock in the morning. On nights of prolonged discussion, when the houses sit late, some of the reporters, particularly those whose previous task may have proved least onerous, are required to return to the gallery, and take what is called "a double turn." In general, however, owing to the subdivision of labour, the duty of an individual reporter is by no means burdensome, and requires promptitude and facility rather than prolonged exertion. The expertness produced by habit is remarkable, and it not unfrequently happens that a single reporter, from the notes taken in three quarters of an hour, supplies from one to three columns of printed matter to the paper on which he is engaged. Besides the corps of regular reporters attached to a newspaper, there are several occasional ones, called "penny-a-line men," from the circumstances of their furnishing articles of intelligence at a fixed price per line. The reporters of this class are to the body of the press what the Cossacks are to a disciplined army; a species of active but irregular troops, who forage for news in all directions, pick up every scrap that comes in their way, and having dressed it up in their best style, straightway offer it for sale at the newspaper offices.

NEWSPAPERS, seventh edition (1830–42). By James Browne (1793–1841), journalist and author, editor of the *Scots Magazine* and then of the *Caledonian Mercury*.

Abridgement

Abridgement, in literature, a term signifying the reduction of a book into a smaller compass.—The art of conveying much sentiment in few words, is the happiest talent an author can be possessed of. This talent is peculiarly necessary in the present state of literature; for many writers have acquired the dexterity of spreading a few critical thoughts over several hundred pages. When an author hits upon a thought that pleases him, he is apt to dwell upon it, to view it in different lights, to force it in improperly, or upon the slightest relations. Though this may be pleasant to the writer, it tires and vexes the reader. There is another great source of diffusion in composition. It is a capital object with an author, whatever be the subject, to give vent to all his best thoughts. When he finds a proper place for any of them, he is peculiarly happy. But, rather than sacrifice a thought he is fond of, he forces it in by way of digression, or superfluous illustration. If none of these expedients answer his purpose, he has recourse to the margin, a very convenient apartment for all manner of pedantry and impertinence. There is not an author, however correct, but is more or less faulty in this respect. An abridger, however, is not subject to these temptations. The thoughts are not his own; he views them in a cooler and less affectionate manner; he discovers an impropriety in some, a vanity in others, and a want of utility in many. His business, therefore, is to retrench superfluities, digressions, quotations, pedantry, *etc.* and to lay before the public only what is really useful. This is by no means an easy employment: To abridge some books, requires talents equal, if not superior, to those of the author. The facts, manner, spirit, and reasoning, must be preserved; nothing essential, either in argument or illustration, ought to be omitted. The difficulty of the task is the principal reason why we have so few good abridgements: Wynne's abridgement of Locke's Essay on the Human Understanding is, perhaps, the only unexceptionable one in our language. . . .

Abridging is peculiarly useful in taking the substance of what is delivered by Professors, *etc.* Every public speaker has circumlocutions, redundancies, lumber, which deserve not to be copied. All that is really useful may be comprehended in a short compass. If the plan of the discourse, and arguments employed in support of the different branches be taken down, you have the whole. These you may afterwards extend in the form of a discourse dressed in your own language. This would not only be a more rational employment, but would likewise be an excellent method of improving young men in composition, an object too little attended to in all our universities. Besides, it would be more for the honour of professors; as it would prevent at least such immense loads of disjointed and unintelligible rubbish from being handed about by the name of such a man's lectures.

ABRIDGEMENT, first edition (1768–71).

Poetry

Poetry is an art where every thing should please. It is not enough to exhibit nature, which in certain places and circumstances is rude and unpleasant; but the poet must chuse in her what is beautiful from what is not: whence a poet ought to chuse, for the subject of his imitation, something naturally affecting. . . .

In fine, to accomplish a poet, is required a temperature of wit and fancy, of strength and sweetness, of penetration and delicacy; but, above all, he must have a sovereign eloquence, and a profound capacity. These are the qualities that must concur together to form the genius of a poet, and sustain his character.

POETRY, first edition (1768–71).

The above illustration is fig. 29, Upper and Lower Jaws and Teeth of the Wolf-fish (Anarchias lupus), half natural size, from ODONTOLOGY, *by Sir Richard Owen in the eighth edition (1853–60). This article on teeth runs to 78 pages and is illustrated with 146 separate figures. Sir Richard Owen, Fellow of the Royal Society, was superintendent of the Natural History department of the British museum and was a pioneer in vertebrate palaeontology.*

On Composition

It is with thoughts, as it is with words; and with both, as with men, they may grow old and die. Words tarnished, by passing through the mouths of the vulgar, are laid aside as inelegant and obsolete. So thoughts, when become too common, should lose their currency; and we should send new metal to the mint, that is, new meaning to the press. . . .

After all, the first ancients had not merit in being *originals*: they could *not* be *imitators*. Modern writers have a *choice* to make; and therefore have a merit in their power. They may soar in the regions of *liberty*, or move in the soft fetters of easy *imitation*; and *imitation* has as many plausible reasons to urge, as *pleasure* had to offer to Hercules. Hercules made the choice of an hero, and *so* became immortal.

Must we, then, not imitate ancient authors? Imitate them, by all means; but imitate aright. He that imitates the divine Iliad, does not imitate Homer; but he who takes the same method, which Homer took, for arriving at a capacity of accomplishing a work so great. Tread in his steps to the sole fountain of immortality; drink where he drank, at the true *Helicon*, that is, at the breast of nature. Imitate, but imitate not the *composition*, but the *man*. For may not this paradox pass into a maxim? *viz*. "The less we copy the renowned ancients, we shall resemble them the more."

COMPOSITION, first edition (1768–71).

On Poetic Diction

The true poet must not only study nature and know the reality of things, but must also possess fancy, to invent additional decorations; judgement, to direct him in the choice of such as accord with verisimilitude; and sensibility, to enter with ardent emotions into every part of his subject, so as to transfuse into every part of his work a pathos and energy sufficient to raise correspondent emotions in the reader. . . .

One mode of improvement peculiar to poetical diction results from the use of those words and phrases which, because they rarely occur in prose, and frequently in verse, are by the grammarian and lexicographer termed *poetical*. . . .

We must not suppose that these poetical words never occur at all except in poetry. Even from conversation they are not excluded: and the ancient critics allow, that they may be admitted into prose, where they occasionally confer dignity upon a sublime subject, or heighten the ludicrous qualities of a mean one. But it is in poetry only where the frequent use of them does not savour of affectation. . . .

Many passages there are of exquisite poetry, wherein not a single phrase occurs that might not be used in prose. In fact, the influence of these words in adorning English verse is not very extensive. Some influence however they have. They serve to render the poetical style, first, more melodious; and secondly, more solemn.

Tropes and figures are often necessary to supply the unavoidable defects of language. When *proper* words are wanting, or not recollected, or when we do not choose to be always repeating them, we must have recourse to tropes and figures. . . . And hence another use of figurative language, that it contributes to poetical harmony. Thus, to *press the plain*, is frequently used to signify to *be slain in battle*; *liquid plain* is put for *ocean*, *blue serene* for *sky*, and *sylvan reign* for *country life*. . . .

The delicacy we here contend for, may indeed, both in conversation and in writing, be carried too far. To call *killing an innocent man in a duel* an affair of honour, and *a violation of the rights of wedlock* an affair of gallantry, is a prostitution of figurative language.

POETRY, second edition (1777–83).

Pope's Place as a Poet

Not therefore for superior correctness, but for qualities the very same as belong to his most distinguished brethren, is Pope to be considered a great poet; for impassioned thinking, powerful description, pathetic reflection, brilliant narration. His characteristic difference is simply that he carried these powers into a different field, and moved chiefly amongst the social paths of men, and viewed their characters as operating through their manners. And our obligations to him arise chiefly on this ground, that having already, in the persons of earlier poets, carried off the palm in all the grander trials of intellectual strength, for the majesty of the epopee and the impassioned vehemence of the tragic drama, to Pope we owe it that we can now claim an equal pre-eminence in the sportive and aerial graces of the mock heroic and satiric muse; that in the Dunciad we possess a peculiar form of satire, in which (according to a plan unattempted by any other nation) we see alternatively her festive smile and her gloomiest scowl; that the grave good sense of the nation has here found its brightest mirror; and, finally, that through Pope the cycle of our poetry is perfected and made orbicular, that from that day we might claim the laurel equally, whether for dignity or grace.

POPE, ALEXANDER, seventh edition (1830–42). By Thomas De Quincey (1785–1859), writer and literary critic, author of *Confessions of an English Opium-Eater* (1822).

S. T. Coleridge

Coleridge's whole mind was imbued with the love of truth and of beauty; for truth he wandered through the mazes of all philosophy, and wherever he found her, he grappled her to his soul with hooks of steel. When an extended horizon of Christianity enabled him to see the real position of his Socinian opinion, he embraced unchangeably with his whole heart "the truth as it is in Jesus." The very obscurities of Coleridge are "dark with excessive bright;" from his intense feeling of the beautiful, they are "golden mists" that rise from the morning of a pure heart; or they are lucid seas whose very depth prevents the eye from penetrating its extent. His prose style is disfigured by turgidity, and the affected use of words. His written humour is ponderous and unwieldly.

He was capable of immense services to poetry; but in this, as in other spheres of labour, he lived on the future; and Coleridge's future was a bad bank on which to draw; its bills were perpetually dishonoured. The conspicuous features of his poetry are its exquisite and original melody of versification, whose very sound chains the ear and soul; the harmonious grouping and skilful colouring of his pictures; statuesqueness and purity of taste in his living figures, and truth, in luxuriance or in simplicity, in majesty or in smallness, in his descriptions of nature. In sentiment, he opens with charming artlessness his own bosom in sorrow and in joy; this, it may be remarked, is a feature characteristic of the poetry of our own age above all that have preceded. There exists in general a decided contrast between the simplicity and lucidness of Coleridge's poetical style of expression, and the involved cloud-like fashion of his prose. Apart from his German translations and his dramas, there are few compositions of any extent complete in the works of Coleridge. "Christabel" is a fragment—a beauteous strain creeping in the ear, mysterious yet enrapturing as a celestial melody; but the import of whose language we scarcely comprehend, while we feel its sweetness. Capriciously it ceases in a moment, and leaves us in the position of Ariel's admirers in the tune played by the picture of nobody.

COLERIDGE, SAMUEL TAYLOR, eighth edition (1853–60). By Thomas De Quincey (1785–1859), writer and literary critic, author of *Confessions of an English Opium-Eater* (1822).

William Wordsworth

English poet . . . This enthusiastic worshipper of nature and simplicity resided for about half a century in the picturesque lake-country in Westmoreland, and gave forth his poetical oracles, as the great Pan of the lakes, with unfaltering confidence and power. He was long neglected, ridiculed, and condemned; but he lived to see his creed widely adopted and firmly established. He never sank into apathy nor despondency, but dignified his retirement by the careful cultivation of his intellectual powers, and by the lustre of a blameless and unspotted life. Without the force and splendour of Byron, the universality of Scott, the chastened energy and melodious pathos of Campbell, or the sparkling brilliancy of Moore, Wordsworth was more original and philosophical than any of his great contemporaries, and he has sent forth strains that recall the divine genius of Milton. He was not without grievous faults. His taste was not equal to his genius; the power or the will to discriminate, reject, and condense, was wanting. He brooded over his poetical conceptions and theories with a fond and undistinguishing partiality, that extended to puerilities and

conceits, no less than to his loftiest and most profound speculations. This error lay upon the surface, and was peculiarly open to satire. It was not prominent, however, in his later and most finished productions; and those higher flights kept possession of the better part of the public. By repeated efforts, he stamped his mind upon the age, and his influence promises to be lasting. . . . The rise of Wordsworth's reputation, in spite of every obstacle, in the face of a dazzling file of competitors, and in defiance of hostile criticism, furnishes a remarkable proof of the purer taste and elevated moral feeling that have, during the last half century, gained ground among the readers of poetry, and of that love of nature and that kindred sympathy with humanity, even in its lowliest forms, which it was the great and unceasing business of his life to inculcate.

WORDSWORTH, WILLIAM, eighth edition (1853–60). By R. Carruthers (1799–1878), a distinguished Scottish man of letters and notable editor.

French Atheism

Of the prevalence of atheism at Paris, among the higher classes, at the period of which we are now speaking, the *Memoirs* and *Correspondance* of the Baron de Grimm afford the most unquestionable proofs. His friend Diderot seems to have been one of its most zealous abettors; who, it appears from various accounts, contributed to render it fashionable, still more by the extraordinary powers of his conversation, than by the odd combination of eloquence and of obscurity displayed in all his metaphysical productions.

In order, however, to prevent misapprehension of my meaning, it is proper for me to caution my readers against supposing that *all* the eminent French philosophers of this period were of the same school with Grimm and Diderot. On this subject many of our English writers have been misled by taking for granted that to speak lightly of final causes is, of itself, sufficient proof of atheism. That this is a very rash as well as uncharitable conclusion, no other proof is necessary than the manner in which final causes are spoken of by Descartes himself, the great object of whose metaphysical writings plainly was, to establish by demonstration the existence of God. . . .

As to the unqualified charge of atheism, which has been brought by some French ecclesiastics against all of their countrymen that have presumed to differ from the tenets of the Catholic church, it will be admitted, with large allowances, by every candid Presbyterian, when it is recollected that something of the same illiberality formerly existed under the comparatively enlightened establishment of England. In the present times, the following anecdote would appear incredible, if it did not rest on the unquestionable testimony of Dr Jortin: "I hear Dr B. say in a sermon, if any one denies the uninterrupted succession of bishops, I shall not scruple to call him a downright atheist. This, when I was young (Jortin adds), was sound, orthodox, and fashionable doctrine." (*Tracts*, Vol. I. p. 436.)

How far the effects of that false philosophy of which Grimm's correspondence exhibits so dark and so authentic a picture, were connected with the awful revolution which soon after followed, it is not easy to say. That they contributed greatly to blacken its atrocities, as well as to revolt against it the feelings of the whole Christian world, cannot be disputed. The experiment was indeed tremendous, to set loose the passions of all classes of men from the restraints imposed by religious principles; and the result exceeded, if possible, what could have been anticipated in theory. The lesson it has afforded has been dearly purchased; but let us indulge the hope that it will not be thrown away on the generations which are to come.

DISSERTATION: *exhibiting a general view of the Progress of Metaphysical, Ethical and Political Philosophy*, supplement to the fourth, fifth and sixth editions (1816–24). By Dugald Stewart (1753–1828), the Scottish philosopher, member of the Royal Societies of London and Edinburgh and professor of moral philosophy at Edinburgh university. He was so greatly admired that, while the continent of Europe was closed to Englishmen during the Napoleonic Wars, it was customary to send young men to Edinburgh in order to attend his lectures, as a substitute for the "grand tour."

An Experiment in Steam by James Watt

In the winter of 1764–5, I made experiments at Glasgow on the subject, in the course of my endeavours to improve the steam-engine, and as I did not then think of any *simple* method of trying the elasticities of steam at temperatures less than that of boiling water, and had at hand a digester by which the elasticities at greater heats could be tried, I considered that, by establishing the ratios in which they proceeded, the elasticities at lower heats might be found nearly enough for my purpose. I therefore fitted a thermometer to the digester, with its bulb in the inside, placed a small cistern with mercury also within the digester, fixed a small barometer tube with its end in the mercury, and left the upper end open. I then made the digester boil for some time, the steam issuing at the safety-valve, until the air contained in the digester was supposed to be expelled. The safety-valve being shut, the steam acted upon the surface of the mercury in the cistern, and made it rise in the tube. When it reached to 15 inches above the surface of the mercury in the cistern, the heat was 236°; and at 30 inches above that surface, the heat was 252°. Here I was obliged to stop, as I had no tube longer than 34 inches, and there was no white glass made nearer than Newcastle-upon-Tyne. I therefore sealed the upper end of the tube hermetically, whilst it was empty, and when it was cool immersed the lower end in the mercury, which now could only rise in the tube by compressing the air it contained. The tube was somewhat conical; but, by ascertaining how much it was so, and making allowances accordingly, the following points were found, which, though not exact, were tolerably near for an

aperçu. At 29½ inches (with the sealed tube) the heat was 252°, at 75½ inches the heat was 264°, and at 110½ inches 292°. (That is, after making allowances for the pillar of mercury supported, and the pillar which would be necessary to compress the air into the space which it occupied, these were the results.) From these elements I laid down a curve, in which the abscissæ represented the temperatures, and the ordinates the pressures, and thereby found the law by which they were governed, sufficiently near for my then purpose. It was not till the years 1773–4, that I found leisure to make further experiments on this subject.

STEAM, seventh edition (1830–42). The above passage is by James Watt (1736–1819), the famous inventor, who in old age undertook the revision of the classic article by his friend the late Professor Robison (1739–1805; "one of the greatest mathematical philosophers of his age") but was unable to complete his work. When this was done by another hand, some passages of Robison's and Watt's work that were retained were marked with * and † respectively and so can still be identified.

Objection to a Sinking Fund

After having duly considered the operation of a sinking fund, derived from annual taxes, we come now to the consideration of the best mode of providing for our annual expenditure, both in war and peace; and, further, to examine whether a country can have any security, that a fund raised for the purpose of paying debt will not be misapplied by ministers, and be really made the instrument for creating new debt, so as never to afford a rational hope that any progress whatever will permanently be made in the reduction of debt.

Suppose a country to be free from debt, and a war to take place, which should involve it in an annual additional expenditure of twenty millions, there are three modes by which this expenditure may be provided; first, taxes may be raised to the amount of twenty millions *per annum*, from which the country would be totally freed on the return of peace; or, secondly, the money might be annually borrowed and funded; in which case, if the interest agreed upon was 5 *per cent.*, a perpetual charge of one million *per annum* taxes would be incurred for the first year's expence, from which there would be no relief during peace, or in any future war; of an additional million for the second year's expence, and so on for every year that the war might last. At the end of twenty years, if the war lasted so long, the country would be perpetually encumbered with taxes of twenty millions *per annum*, and would have to repeat the same course on the recurrence of any new war. The third mode of providing for the expences of the war would be to borrow annually the twenty millions required as before, but to provide, by taxes, a fund, in addition to the interest, which, accumulating at compound interest, should finally be equal to the debt. . . .

Of these three modes, we are decidedly of opinion that the preference should be given to the first. The burthens of the war are undoubtedly great during its continuance, but at its termination they cease altogether. When the pressure of the war is felt at once, without mitigation, we shall be less disposed wantonly to engage in an expensive contest, and if engaged in it, we shall be sooner disposed to get out of it, unless it be a contest for some great national interest. . . .

We are now to compare the other two modes of defraying the expences of a war, one by borrowing the capital expended, and providing annual taxes permanently for the payment of the interest, the other by borrowing the capital expended, and besides providing the interest by annual taxes, raising, by the same mode, an additional revenue (and which is called the sinking fund), with a view, within a certain determinate time, to redeem the original debt, and get rid entirely of the taxes.

Under the firm conviction that nations will at last adopt the plan of defraying their expences, ordinary and extraordinary, at the time they are incurred, we are favourable to every plan which shall soonest redeem us from debt; but then we must be convinced that the plan is effective for the object. This then is the place to examine whether we have, or can have, any security for the due application of the sinking fund to the payment of debt. . . .

It is, we think, sufficiently proved, that no securities can be given by ministers that the sinking fund shall be faithfully devoted to the payment of debt, and without such securities we should be much better without such a fund. To pay off the whole, or a great portion of our debt, is, in our estimation, a most desirable object; if, at the same time, we acknowledged the evils of the funding system, and resolutely determined to carry on our future contests without having recourse to it. This cannot, or rather will not, be done by a sinking fund as at present constituted, nor by any other that we can suggest; but if, without raising any fund, the debt were paid by a tax on property, once for all, it would effect its object. Its operation might be completed in two or three years during peace; and, if we mean honestly to discharge the debt, we do not see any other mode of accomplishing it.

FUNDING SYSTEM, supplement to the fourth, fifth and sixth editions (1816–24). By David Ricardo (1772–1823), economist, who systematized the rising science of economics. [The sinking

fund system, established after the South Sea bubble in 1720, was a method of accumulating money for the payment of government debt by the appropriation of certain taxes. The 1963 printing of the *Encyclopaedia Britannica* in the article GREAT BRITAIN says: "Sir Robert Walpole established a sinking fund of £1,000,000 a year, but it was often raided both by himself and his successors. In 1786, William Pitt the younger provided that £1,000,000 a year was to be paid to commissioners for the reduction of the national debt. They were to buy government stock (bonds), which was not to be cancelled but to be held by them, and the interest was to be used to make further purchases. However, the plan had been in operation only seven years when it was overwhelmed by the immense new borrowings caused by the wars of 1793–1815."]

Speculative Character of the Crédit Mobilier

The government of Louis Napoleon has been compelled to ally itself rather closely with wealth, and especially with newly-made commercial wealth. The single defence of the *coup d'état* was the necessity of preserving industry and credit from the attacks of multitudes, who, either from bad theories or bad motives, were anxious for a new distribution of property. The trading class, who live by their industry and their credit, were influenced by this argument, and leaned towards the new government. The classes connected with the former governments of France were naturally disinclined to it. The legitimist noblesse could not approve the revival of the Bonapartist dynasty; the literary and oratorical statesmen of the Orleanist monarchy could find no place for their characteristic abilities in a government which enforced a silence on parliamentary eloquence and on newspaper eloquence, which did not wish to be supported by abstract speculations which only valued administrative ability. These are the natural results of human nature. It is, perhaps, equally so that the class of mercantile men who would most rally round a court, would not be the highest class. A close proximity to a gorgeous gaiety does not suit a sober and stable industry. The eager speculator who is in haste to be rich, in order that he may spend his riches, will seek the scenes of expenditure the moment he is thought to have riches. From causes such as these, the imperial government of France has been obliged to surround itself with a certain class of speculators rarely found in palaces, without a greater check from men of higher cultivation and more stable opulence. It has been contended that the Crédit Mobilier, which has been avowedly patronized by the imperial government, is in reality a speculation of these courtiers.

MOBILIER, CRÉDIT, eighth edition (1853–60). By Walter Bagehot (1826–77), economist, political analyst and sociologist. [The 1963 printing of the *Encyclopaedia Britannica* states: "The Crédit Foncier and the Crédit Mobilier were both formed in 1852; both did a limited deposit business, but the former was chiefly an agricultural mortgage company and the latter an investment bank. The Crédit Mobilier after a spectacular career, was liquidated in 1867, but the Crédit Foncier remained an important part of the French financial system."]

Long Horned Bull.

Short Horned Bull.

Long-horned bull (top) *and short-horned bull, from* AGRICULTURE, *supplement to the fourth, fifth and sixth editions* (1816-24)

British Coinage

British coinage, both by the beauty of the engraving, and by the invention of the impressions on the edges, that admirable expedient for preventing the alteration of the species, is carried to the utmost perfection. . . .

The British coinage is now wholly performed in the Tower of London, where there is a corporation for it, under the title of the mint. Formerly there were here, as there are still in other countries, the rights of seinorage and brassage: but since the eighteenth year of king Charles the Second, there is nothing taken either for the king, or for the expences of coining; so that weight is returned for weight, to any person who carries their gold and silver to the Tower.

The species coined in Great Britain are esteemed contraband goods, and not to be exported. All foreign species are allowed to be sent out of the realm, as well as gold and silver in bars, ingots, dust, etc.

COINAGE, first edition (1768–71).

To Counterfeit Emeralds

Take of natural crystal, four ounces; of red-lead, four ounces; verdegrease, forty-eight grains; crocus martis, prepared with vinegar, eight grains; let the whole be finely pulverized and sifted; put this into a crucible, leaving one inch empty; lute it well, and put it into a potter's furnace, and let it stand there as long as they do their pots. When cold, break the crucible, and you will find a matter of a fine emerald colour, which, after it is cut and set in gold, will surpass in beauty an oriental emerald.

EMERALD, first edition (1768–71).

A Card Trick

On the ace of spades fix, with soap, a heart, and on the ace of hearts, a spade, in such a manner that they will not easily slip off.

Show these two aces to the company; then taking the ace of spades, you desire a person to put his foot upon it, and as you place it on the ground, draw away the spade. In like manner you place the seeming ace of hearts under the foot of another person. You then command the two cards to change their places; and that they obey your commands, the two persons, on taking up their cards, will have ocular demonstration. A deception similar to this is sometimes practised with one card, suppose the ace of spades, over which a heart is placed slightly. After showing a person the card, you let him hold one end of it, and you hold the other, and while you amuse him with discourse, you slide off the heart. Then laying the card on the table, you bid him cover it with his hand. You then knock under the table and command the heart to turn into the ace of spades. By deceptions like these, people of little ex-

perience and much conceit are frequently deprived of their money, and rendered ridiculous.

LEGERDEMAIN, second edition (1777–83).

How to Calculate Odds for "Doubles"

Again, suppose I have two wagers depending, in the first of which I have 3 to 2 the best of the lay, and in the second 7 to 4, what is the probability I win both wagers?

The probability of winning the first is 3/5, that is the number of chances I have to win, divided by the number of all the chances: the probability of winning the second is 7/11: therefore, multiplying these two fractions together, the product will be 21/55, which is the probability of winning both wagers. Now, this fraction being subtracted from 1, the remainder is 34/55, which is the probability I do not win both wagers: therefore the odds against me are 34 to 21.

GAMING, first edition (1768–71).

Against Unreasonably Severe Punishments

Lastly, as a conclusion to the whole, we may observe, that punishments of unreasonable severity, especially when indiscriminately inflicted, have less effect in preventing crimes, and amending the manners of a people, than such as are more merciful in general, yet properly intermixed with due distinctions of severity. It is the sentiment of an ingenious writer, who seems to have well studied the springs of human action, that crimes are more effectually prevented by the certainty than by the severity of punishment; for the excessive severity of laws (says Montesquieu) hinders their execution. When the punishment surpasses all measure, the public will frequently prefer impunity to it. . . . We may further observe, that sanguinary laws are a bad symptom of the distemper of any state, or at least of its weak constitution. The laws of the Roman kings, and the twelve tables of the *decemviri*, were full of cruel punishments: the Porcian law, which exempted all citizens from sentence of death, silently abrogated them all. In this period the republic flourished: under the emperors severe punishments were revived, and then empire fell.

CRIME AND PUNISHMENT, second edition (1777–83).

The Purpose of Imprisonment

The arrangements, necessary to adapt prisons to the ends for which they are designed, seem to require little more than the exercise of practical good sense; and yet the manner in which the practice of the world blunders on from one absurdity, and very often from one atrocity, to another, shows pretty distinctly, how little the public affairs of mankind have hitherto had the benefit of that practical faculty, or of any thing that resembles it. . . .

Persons in prison before trial, and debtors, are

persons of whom nothing is certainly known, but that they are unfortunate. They are, therefore, entitled to all the benevolence which is due to the unfortunate.

What is done for them in a prison must, however, be done at the expense of the community, that is, by sacrifices demanded of those who are not in prison; and those sacrifices ought, undoubtedly, to be the smallest possible. The question is, therefore, to be settled by a compromise between the principle of benevolence, and the principle of economy.

The principle of benevolence undoubtedly requires that the health of the prisoners should not be impaired; for this, importing the premature loss of life, is in reality the punishment of death, inflicted upon those to whom no punishment is due.

That health may not be impaired, three things are indispensable: 1. A wholesome apartment; 2. A sufficiency of wholesome food; 3. Sufficient clothing.

The principle of economy, with equal certainty, exacts, that all those should be of the cheapest possible kind. . . .

If a criminal in a prison is ever to be let out again, and to mix in society, it is desirable that nothing should be done, and least of all done of purpose, to make him a worse member of society than when he went in. There cannot be a worse quality of punishment, than that it has a tendency to corrupt and deteriorate the individual on whom it is inflicted: unless, indeed, he is a prisoner for life; in that case, people of a certain temper might say, that making worse his disposition is a matter of little importance; and to them we have no time to make any reply.

Most of those persons who come into prison as criminals, are bad, because they have hated labour, and have had recourse to other means than their industry of attaining the supply of their wants and the gratification of their desires. People of industry, people who love labour, seldom become the criminal inmates of a prison.

One thing, however, is pretty certain, that men seldom become in love with their punishments. If the grand cause of the crimes which have brought a man to punishment is his not having a love but hatred of labour; to make labour his punishment, is only to make him hate it the more. If the more a man hates labour, the more he is likely to act as a bad member of society; to punish a man with labour, and then to turn him out upon society, is a course of legislation which savours not of the highest wisdom.

Besides, in treating labour as an instrument of punishment, call it *hard* labour, if you will, what sort of a lesson do you teach to the industrious and laborious class, who form the great body of your people? to those whose lot is labour, whose lot is hard labour, harder than any which it is in your power to impose? What compulsory labour is so hard as many species of voluntary labour?

As an instrument of reformation, labour, as we shall presently see, is invaluable. As an instrument of punishment, hardly any thing can be conceived more

exceptionable. That which is the source of all that mankind enjoy, that which is the foundation of every virtue in the most numerous class of the community, would you stamp with ignominy and dishonour, by inflicting it as a punishment upon the worst and basest of your people? Is this your expedient for rendering it, what every wise legislator would wish to render it, honourable, and thence desirable? . . .

1. The grand object, as we have stated, of reformatory discipline is, to create habits of useful industry.

2. A second object is, to preserve the health of the prisoners, and impose upon them no suffering, not implied in the conditions of their confinement, or prescribed by the judge.

3. A third is, by moral and religious tuition, to generate and strengthen good dispositions.

4. A fourth is, to attain those ends at the smallest possible expense.

PRISONS AND PRISON DISCIPLINE, supplement to the fourth, fifth and sixth editions (1816–24). The brief extracts above are taken from the article by James Mill (1773–1836), historian, economist and philosopher, and father of John Stuart Mill. [The article was so highly thought of that the editors reproduced it in the seventh edition, with the following note: "The preceding article has been preserved entire, as having been the offspring of a very powerful mind, and as presenting a perspicuous outline of the most advanced ideas of a good system of prison discipline, which prevailed up to the time of its publication (April 1823)." Mill's theories on prison discipline are those of Jeremy Bentham (1748–1832) who drew up a scheme for a model prison, the "Panopticon", based on the principles of philosophic radicalism.]

A Method of Removing Foul Air from Jails

The air-trunk is also a contrivance by Dr. Hales to prevent the stagnation of putrid effluvia in jails, and other places where a great number of people are crowded together in a small space. It consists only of a long square trunk open at both ends; one of which is inserted into the ceiling of the room, the air of which is required to be kept pure; and the other extends a good way beyond the roof. Through this trunk a continued circulation is carried on: and the reason is, that the putrid effluvia which do so much mischief when collected, being much lighter than the pure atmosphere, arise to the top of the room; and, if they there find a vent, will continually go out through it. These effluvia arise in very considerable quantity, being calculated by the late Dr. Keil at no less than 39 ounces from one man in 24 hours.

AIR, fourth edition (1800–10).

Prison is Custody, not Punishment

Prison, a gaol, or place of confinement. Lord Coke observes, that a prison is only a place of safe custody, *salva custodia*, not a place of punishment. If this be so, and it cannot be questioned, prisons ought not to be, what they are in most parts of Europe, loathsome dungeons.

PRISON, third edition (1788–97).

Politeness

Politeness means elegance of manners or good breeding: Lord Chesterfield calls it the art of pleasing. It has also been called an artificial good nature; and indeed good nature is the foundation of true politeness; without which art will make but a very indifferent figure, and will generally defeat its own ends. . . .

It is the dictate of humanity, that we should endeavour to render ourselves agreeable to those in whose company we are destined to travel in the journey of life. It is our interest, it is the source of perpetual satisfaction; it is one of our most important duties as men, and particularly required in the professor of Christianity. . . .

The qualities essential in the art of pleasing, are *virtue, knowledge,* and *manners*. All the virtues which form a good and respectable character in a moral sense are essential to the art of pleasing. This must be an established principle, because it depends on the wants and mutual relations of society. In all affairs of common business, we delight in transacting with men in whom we can place confidence, and in whom we find integrity; but truth is so naturally pleasing, and the common affairs of life are so interwoven with social intercourse, that we derive abundantly more satisfaction from an honest character than from specious manners. . . .

Genuine easy manners result from a constant attention to the relations of persons, things, time, and places.

POLITENESS, fourth edition (1800–10).

Actresses

Actresses are said not to have been introduced on the English stage till after the restoration of King Charles II. who has been charged with contributing to the corrupting of our manners by importing this usage from abroad. But this can be but partly true: the queen of James I. acted a part in a pastoral; and Prynn, in his Histriomastix, speaks of women actors in his time as prostitutes; which was one occasion of the severe prosecution brought against him for that book.

There are some very agreeable and beautiful talents, of which the possession commands a certain sort of admiration; but of which the exercise for the sake of gain is considered, whether from reason or prejudice, as a sort of public prostitution. The pecuniary recompense, therefore, of those who exercise them in this manner, must be sufficient, not only to pay for the time, labour, and expense of acquiring the talents, but for the discredit which attends the employment of them as the means of subsistence. The exorbitant rewards of players, opera-singers, opera-dancers, etc. are founded upon these two principles; the rarity and beauty of the talents, and the discredit, of employing them in this manner. It seems absured at first sight that we should despise their persons, and yet reward their talents with the most profuse liberality. While we do the one, however, we must of necessity do the other. Should the public opinion or prejudice ever alter with regard to such occupations, their pecuniary recompense would quickly diminish. More people would apply to them, and the competition would quickly reduce the price of their labour. Such talents, though far from being common, are by no means so rare as is imagined. Many people possess them in great perfection, who disdain to make this use of them; and many more are capable of acquiring them, if any thing could be made honourably by them.

ACTRESS, fourth edition (1800–10).

The Tarantula Spider

The tarantula spider. The breast (1), and belly (2), are of an ash-colour; the legs (3) are likewise ash-coloured, with blackish rings on the under part; the fangs, or nippers (4), are red on the inner side, the rest being blackish; (5) is the antennæ or feelers: Two of its eyes are larger than the other, red, and placed in the

ARANEA TARANTULA

front; four other eyes are placed in a transverse direction towards the mouth; the other two are nearer the back. It is a native of Italy, Cyprus, Barbary, and the E. Indies. The breast and belly are about two inches long, terminated by two short tails. This figure was taken from the life, in the island of Cyprus, by Alexr. Drummond, Esq; late consul at Aleppo. The bite of the tarantula is said to occasion an inflammation in the part, which in a few hours brings on sickness, fainting, and difficulty of breathing: The person afterwards is affected with a delirium, putting himself into the most extravagant postures. However, this is not always the case; for they are sometimes seized with a deep melancholy. The same symptoms return annually, in some cases, for several years, and at last terminate in death. Music is said to be the only cure. It induces the patient to dance, and sweat out the poison. [The symptoms recorded above were not the result of the spider's bite, which, although poisonous, is now known not to be dangerous to man.]

ARANEA, first edition (1768–71).

Abstinence in Serpents

Among the inferior animals, we see extraordinary instances of long abstinence. The serpent kind, in particular, bear abstinence to a wonderful degree. We have seen rattle-snakes which had lived many months without any food, yet still retained their vigour and fierceness. Dr. Shaw speaks of a couple of cerastes (a sort of Egyptian serpents), which had been kept five years in a bottle close corked, without any sort of food, unless a small quantity of sand in which they coiled themselves up in the bottom of the vessel may be reckoned as such: yet when he saw them they had newly cast their skins, and were as brisk and lively as if just taken.

ABSTINENCE, fourth edition (1800–10).

Caprimulgus, or Nightjar

CAPRIMULGUS, Goat-sucker, or Fern-owl, in ornithology, a genus of birds belonging to the order of passers. The beak is incurvated, small, tapering, and depressed at the base; the hairs at the mouth, which it opens very wide, are placed in a row. There are two species, viz. Europæus, with the tubes of the nostrils hardly visible. It is a native of Europe, and feeds upon moths and nocturnal insects. This bird is said to suck goats in the night. The Americanus, has the tubes of the nostrils very conspicuous. This is a night-bird, and is found in America.

CAPRIMULGUS, first edition (1768–71).

CAPRIMULGUS, or Goat Sucker.

Phlebotomy, or the Practice of Bleeding

We begin with the operation of phlebotomy: because it is of all the most general, performed in most parts of the body, and by much the most frequent in use at this present day. By phlebotomy, or bleeding, we here intend the opening a vein, by a sharp-edged and pointed instrument of steel, for extracting a proper quantity of blood, either for the preservation or recovery of a person's health. . . .

There are several things worthy the surgeon's notice in this operation; some of which regard the things which are to be done preparatory to bleeding, some in the operation itself, others immediately after the performance of it. Preparatory to bleeding you should have in readiness: (1) A linen fillet, about an ell in length, and two fingers in breadth. (2) Two small square bolsters. (3) Porringers or vessels to receive the blood. (4) A sponge with warm water. (5) Some vinegar, wine, or Hungary water, to raise the patient's spirits if he should be inclinable to faint. (6) Two assistants one to hold the porringer, the other to reach you anything that you shall want. (7) You must place your patient upon a couch; or, if he is very fearful of the operation, lay him upon a bed, lest he should fall into a swoon. . . .

It is necessary for the surgeon to inspect his patient's arm diligently, that he may see the course of the veins: he must then take hold of the arm, and extend it towards his breast, tucking up the sleeve about a hand's breadth above the bend of the cubit, where he must make his ligature, rolling the fillet twice round, and fastening it with a knot. When you have bound up the arm in this manner, you let it go for a small time till the veins grow turgid. You are then to lay hold of the arm again in the same manner as we directed before, and extend it to your breast, having an assistant ready with the vessel in his hand, at a convenient distance for receiving the blood. . . .

When you have determined which vein to open, you are to perform the operation on that part which presents itself fairest to you. But if the vein has frequently been opened, and the part which appears largest and fairest is full of cicatrices, you are not to open above, but below the cicatrices, by which means the blood will discharge itself more freely: For the part above is generally straitened by the cicatrix.

Before you apply the lancet to the skin, when the veins are not risen, it will be proper to rub the arm below the bandage, which will drive the blood back towards the cubit, and render the veins more turgid. Whilst this is doing in the right arm, the surgeon should take hold of the patient's arm in such a manner that he may lay his thumb upon the vein he intends to open, to prevent the blood from flowing back, and to keep the vein from rolling. Taking the lancet with your right hand, so placed that the thumb and first finger may be fixed about the middle of the blade; the other fingers should rest gently upon the patient's arm, to prevent your hand from slipping.

Your lancet is now to be pushed lightly and carefully

forward by your thumb and fore-finger, till it has penetrated through the coats of the vein; and at that instant to be raised a little upwards, in order to enlarge the orifice of the wound, which will give a freer passage to the blood. The most common and convenient size of an orifice is about twice the breadth of the back of an ordinary knife. You are to keep even between the two extremes of rashness and timidity in making the puncture. For as in one case you will only divide the common integuments, and so leave your work undone; so in the other you will run the risque of wounding the artery, nerve, or tendon. . . .

There are many physicians and surgeons, who think that bleeding by the veins of the forehead and temples is much more serviceable and expeditious in relieving all disorders of the head, such as violent pains, vertigo, delirium, melancholy, and raving madness, &c. than the like discharge by veins more remote from the parts affected; judging that their vicinity renders them more capable of evacuating the offending matter of the disease.

SURGERY, first edition (1768–71). [This was an early "classic" article in the *Encyclopaedia Britannica*, treating its subject at length.]

Treatment of Insanity

Public asylums, indeed, existed in most of the metropolitan cities of Europe; but the insane were more generally, if at all troublesome, confined in jails, where they were chained in the lowest dungeons, or made the butts and menials of the most debased criminals. Even in the public asylums, many of which were endowed by the munificence of philanthropists, the inmates were generally confined in low and damp cellars, sometimes isolated in cages or chained to the floor or wall; if harmless, they were huddled together, without regard to their habits, in cells not fitted to contain one tithe of the number immured in them. The medical treatment consisted, perhaps, in an annual bleeding and a few emetics; while the lash was systematically used, justified, and even recommended, as it had been by such authorities as the celebrated William Cullen. These unhappy victims of disease were exhibited to the public like wild beasts, and their passions irritated to gratify a morbid and vulgar curiosity. They were often killed by the ignorance and brutality of their keepers, sometimes during rough methods of forcing meat into them, sometimes by barbarous and violent beating. . . .

In concluding this brief historical retrospect, we cannot refrain from expressing our surprise that the study of mental diseases has been deemed of so little interest or importance hitherto, as to form no part of the curriculum of medical education in this country. Although the large metropolitan asylums afford ample means of illustrating courses of instruction in psychological medicine, the study of the subject has never been required by our licensing medical or surgical boards or universities. Lectures on mental diseases, both systematic and practical, have indeed been delivered in many of the continental medical schools; and of late years, in some of the large asylums of London and in that of Edinburgh, clinical lectures have been given; but attendance upon such courses of instruction is voluntary, with the exceptional case of candidates for appointments in the East India Company's service, who have been required during the last four years to attend an asylum for the insane for three months. This neglect seems altogether unaccountable, when we reflect upon the many collateral sciences students of medicine are compelled to master, of comparatively little value to them in actual practice, and the many diseases, accidents, and operations, toxicological and analytical investigations, they are carefully and minutely schooled in, which it may never fall to their lot, in a long life, to see or practise; while insanity, which affects 1 in every 400 or 500 of the population, and which, in some of its states or forms, they can hardly pass a week in medical practice without being consulted about,—often in circumstances requiring great judgment and skill,—is made no part of their medical education at all.

MENTAL DISEASES, eighth edition (1853–60). By David Skae (1814–73), physician, a brilliant specialist in the study and treatment of insanity.

Cranioscopy, or Phrenology

Whence, Dr. Gall [1758–1828] would ask himself, can arise the wide diversity of character and talent among individuals? The solution of this difficult question was not to be hoped for, unless by means of observations conducted on the largest possible scale. He therefore set about examining all the skulls he could lay hold of, that had belonged to individuals whose history was known. He looked out for all persons in any way distinguished for a particular talent or moral quality. He examined their heads with great attention, and noted the peculiarities in their shape. He also collected observations on other individuals, who were remarkable for the weakness of any faculty, and then compared together the positive and negative indications. On the other hand, when he chanced to meet with a head that presented some singularity in shape, he was at much pains to obtain information as to the moral and intellectual character of the person to whom it belonged. When he had no other resource, he did not scruple, as Dr. Spurzheim informs us, to address his questions directly to the person in whose head he observed any distinct protuberance. We are also told, that he was in the habit of collecting around him the boys he met with in the streets of Vienna, and of inducing them, by petty bribes, to confess their own faults, and betray those of their companions. He excited them, for instance, to fight together, in order to discover which possessed most courage, and thence drew inferences as to the organ which prompted that sentiment. In order to obtain more precise data for his conclusions, he endeavoured to procure models of the more remarkable heads that he met with, and generally got permission from the individuals themselves to take a cast of their heads in plaster of Paris. The Count of Sauran, then minister of police at Vienna, gave him material assistance in effecting these objects; and he was thus in no long time in possession of a very large collection of casts, all bearing more or less upon the several points of his theory. If he happened to hear of the death of any one whose head he had already moulded, he was at great pains to procure his skull, that he might compare the form of its different parts with the shape of the head during life. As it was soon known that the doctor aimed chiefly at those who possessed some remarkable talent, a very general alarm spread itself among the inhabitants of Vienna; and not a few were pursued with the terror of being selected as the subjects of cranioscopical investigation, and of their skulls being destined, to make a figure in his anatomical cabinet.

CRANIOSCOPY, supplement to the fourth, fifth and sixth editions (1816–24). By Peter Mark Roget (1779–1869), physician and savant, fellow of the Royal Society of London, and compiler of the *Thesaurus of English Words and Phrases* that bears his name.

A Machine for Draining Ponds without Disturbing the Mud

In figure 1, A is the pipe, loaded with a rim of lead of such weight as serves to sink it below the surface of the water. B is the discharging pipe, laid through the bank HI. C is the joint on which the pipe A turns its form, which is shown fig 2. D is the ball or float, which, swimming on the surface of the pond, prevents

the pipe A from descending deeper than the length of the chain by which they are connected. E is a chain winding on the windlass F, and serving to raise the tube A above the surface of the water, when the machinery is not in use. G is a stage. HI is the bank, represented as if cut through at I, to show the tube B lying within it. K is a post to receive the tube A when lowered, and to prevent it sinking in the mud.

POND, third edition (1788–97).

Napoleon Buonaparte

Posterity will judge of the treatment which Napoleon experienced at the hands of England. A prisoner in another hemisphere, he laboured to defend the reputation which he knew history was preparing for him, and which various parties exaggerated or blackened, according to the dictates of their respective prejudices or passions. But death surprised him at the moment when he was putting his commentaries into shape, and he consequently left them imperfect. They contain much, however, that is not only valuable in itself, but calculated to dispel prejudice, and to throw light upon some of the most important events in his life; and no one can read them attentively without experiencing a feeling of respect and sympathy, mixed with admiration. No man, perhaps, was ever made the object of such unsparing abuse, such bitter detraction, such inveterate and unrelenting rancour; but it is already certain, that neither envy, nor malice, nor hatred, nor slander, will ultimately succeed in depriving him of his just fame. By his victories of Montenotte, Castiglione, Rivoli, the Pyramids, Marengo, Ulm,

Machine for draining Ponds without disturbing the Mud.

Fig. 2   Fig. 1.

Austerlitz, Iena, Friedland, Abensberg, Ratisbon, Wagram, Dresden, Champaubert, Montmirail, and Ligny, he acquired enough of glory to efface the single disaster of Waterloo; and his five codes embody a system of jurisprudence, in the formation of which he had a principal share, and which has not only proved a boon of inestimable value to France, but is even at this day received as authoritative in a great portion of Europe; thus justifying his own proud anticipation, that he would go down to posterity with the codes in his hand.

NAPOLEON BUONAPARTE, seventh edition (1830–42). By James Browne (1793–1841), journalist and author, editor of the *Scots Magazine* and then of the *Caledonian Mercury*.

Alexander the Great

To sum up the character of this prince, we cannot be of opinion, that his good qualities did in anywise compensate for his bad ones. Heroes make a noise; their actions glare, and strike the senses forcibly; while the infinite destruction and misery they occasion lie more in the shade, and out of sight. One good legislator is worth all the heroes that ever did or will exist.

ALEXANDER THE GREAT, fourth edition (1800–10).

Sealing Wafers

Wafers, or Sealing Waffers, are made thus: take very fine flower, mix it with glair of eggs, isinglas, and a little yeast; mingle the materials; beat them well together; spread the batter, being made thin with gum-water; on even tin plates; and dry them in a stove; then cut them out for use.

You may make them of what colour you please, by tinging the paste with brazil or vermilion for red; indigo or verditer, *etc.* for blue; saffron, turmerics, or gambooge, *etc.* for yellow.

WAFERS, first edition (1768–71).

The Proper Clothing of Infants

The absurd mode of swaddling up infants in such a manner as to confine them almost from all motion, and leave scarce a limb at liberty, which has been so often exclaimed against and represented as highly injurious to the symmetry and vigour of the human frame, is now almost entirely laid aside; and therefore we need not raise our voice against it. Still, however, there are certainly too many pins and bandages used in the dress of infants: these are unfavourable to the circulation of the blood, impede the growth, and often occasion those tears and that peevishness which we rashly attribute to the natural ill-humour of the poor creatures. Their dress ought to be loose and cool, so as to press hard on no joint, no vein nor muscle, and to leave every limb at liberty. If too heavy and close, it may occasion too copious a perspiration, and at the same time confine the matter perspired on the surface of the skin; than which nothing can be more prejudicial to the health of the child. It may also, however, be too thin and cool: for as moderate warmth is necessary to the vegetation of plants; so it is no less necessary for promoting the growth of animals: and, therefore, though the dress of infants ought to be loose and easy, yet still it should be moderately warm.

EDUCATION, third edition (1788–97).

The Character of Christ

The character of Christ, as exhibited in the Gospels, presents to us the only example, anywhere to be found, of the perfection of humanity; and the contemplation of it has ever been considered by his followers as one of the most edifying and delightful exercises of piety. A constant regard to the will of God, and a delight in doing it, form the distinguishing features of his character. With this was connected the absence of all sordid, or selfish, or ambitious aims, and an enlarged and enlightened philanthropy. There is perhaps nothing more remarkable in the life of Jesus than the apparently inconsistent qualities which are blended together in one harmonious whole. We see in him the most unbending constancy united with great tenderness of feeling—hatred of sin, and compassion for the offender—a heart superior to all the allurements of pleasure, with a condescending indulgence for the innocent relaxations of life—a mind of universal philanthropy, alive to all the domestic charities—views that extended to the whole human race, and a generous compliance with national and individual peculiarities. It is difficult to conceive that the portraiture presented to us in the sacred history can be contemplated without benefit; but the chief benefit will be lost if it is forgotten that he whose life was the model of every virtue laid down that life for the sins of the world.

JESUS, seventh edition (1830–42). By the Rev. David Welsh (1793–1845), professor of ecclesiastical history at Edinburgh university and moderator of the general assembly of the Church of Scotland, who became a leader of the separatist "general assembly of the Free Protesting Church of Scotland" and was the first moderator of this new body.

The Lord's Prayer in Anglo-Saxon

About the year 900, the Lord's prayer, in the ancient Anglo-Saxon, ran thus:

"Thue ur fader the eart on heofenum, si thin nama gehalgod; cume thin rice si thin willa on eorthan swa, swa on heofenum, etc."

About the year 1160, under Henry II. it was rendered thus by pope Adrian, an Englishman, in rhyme:

"Ure fader in heaven riche,
Thou bring us thy michell blisse:
Als hit in heaven y doe,
Evar in yearth beene it also, *etc.*"

ENGLISH, first edition (1768–71).

INDEX OF EXTRACTS

EXPLANATIONS OF REFERENCES TO TABLES OF MOUNTAINS

As shown on the endpaper at the front of this book

AMERICA.

		Feet.	
1	Nevada de Sorata	25,250	Andes of Peru and Bolivia.
2	Nevada d'Illimani, first peak	24,450	....
3	Ditto, second peak	24,200	....
4	Chimborazo	21,440	....
5	Antisana	19,150	....
6	Cotopaxi	18,890	....
7	Arequipa, volcano	18,373	....
8	Descabeçada	18,000	....
9	Popocateptl	17,716	Mexican chain.
10	Iliniza	17,376	Andes, Bolivia.
11	Citlalpetl, or Peak of Orizaba	17,371	Mexican chain.
12	Tunguragua	16,579	Andes, Bolivia.
13	Nevado de Merida	16,420	Colombia.
14	Cerro de Potosi	16,000	Andes, Bolivia.
15	Pichincha	15,940	....
16	Nevado de Mexico	15,700	Mexican chain.
17	Coffre de Perote	13,514	....
18	Bighorn, or Long's Peak	13,430	Rocky Mountains.
19	Mount St Elias	12,670	....
20	James's Peak	11,500	....
21	Sierra de Cobré	9,000	Cuba.
22	Serrania Grande	9,000	Haiti.
23	Mount Fairweather	8,970	....
24	Duida, volcano	8,467	Colombia.
25	Blue Mountains	7,486	Jamaica.
26	Mount Washington	6,659	White Mountains, U. S.
27	Guadarrama	6,400	Colombia.
28	White Mountains	6,234	New Hampshire.
29	Blaaserk	6,000	East Greenland.
30	Werner Mountains	6,000	....
31	Morne Garou	5,110	St Vincent, W. I.
32	Souffrière	5,041	Guadaloupe, ditto.
33	Moose Hillock	4,636	New Hampshire, U. S.
34	Jorullo, volcano	4,267	Mexico.
35	Pelée	4,260	Martinique, W. I.
36	Camel's Rump	4,188	United States.
37	Saddle Mountain	4,000	....
38	Kaatskill	3,454	New York.
39	Killington Peak	3,450	Vermont.
40	Grand Monadnock	3,254	New Hampshire.
41	Appalachian Peak	2,700	United States.
42	Cape Horn	1,870	Tierra del Fuego.

ASIA AND OCEANICA.

1	Dhawalagiri	26,862	Himalaya.
2	Jewahir	25,749	....
3	Jamautri	25,500	....
4	Dhaibun	24,740	....
5	Hindoo Kho	20,800	....
6	Mowna Kaah	18,400	Owhyhee, or Hawaiah.
7	Elburz	17,796	Caucasus.
8	Agri-dagh, or Ararat.	17,266	Armenia.
9	Klioutsherskoi, volc	16,512	Kamtschatka.
10	Mowna-Roa	16,020	Owhyhee, or Hawaiah.

		Feet.	
11	Kazbec	15,345	Caucasus.
12	Demavend	15,000	Irak.
13	Ophir	13,842	Sumatra.
14	Arjish-dagh, Argæus	13,100	Asia Minor.
15	Gunong Dempu, volc.	12,465	Sumatra.
16	Egmont	11,433	New Zealand.
17	Koriatskaia, volcano	11,215	Kamtschatka.
18	Bielukha	11,000	Altai.
19	Peak	10,895	Otaheite.
20	Italitskoi	10,735	Altai.
21	Krionotskaia, volcano	10,625	Kamtschatka.
22	Shivelutsh, volcano	10,591	....
23	Parmesan	10,050	Banca.
24	Lebanon	9,520	Syria.
25	Awatska, volcano	8,760	Kamtschatka.
26	Dodabetta	8,760	Neilgherries.
27	Daneshken Kamen	8,500?	Ourals.
28	Pedro-galla	8,280	Ceylon.
29	Me-lin	8,200	Quantong, China.
30	Kirrigal Pota	7,810	....
31	Tottapella	7,720	....
32	Peak of Jesso	7,680	Island of Jesso.
33	Sinai	7,500	Arabia Petræa.
34	Adam's Peak	7,420	Ceylon.
35	Olympus	6,500	Asia Minor.
36	Bettigo	6,500	Western Ghauts.
37	Sea-view Hill	6,500	New South Wales.
38	Quelpaert	6,400	Quelpaert Island.
39	Subramani	5,560	Western Ghauts, India.
40	Jebal Akral, or Casius	5,318	Syria.
41	Aboo	5,100	Aravulli, India.
42	Ida	4,960	Asia Minor.
43	Corean Mountains	4,480	Corea.
44	Baskirian Ourals	4,400	Siberia.
45	Benlomond	4,200	Van Diemen's Land.
46	Plain of Ispahan	4,140	Irak, Persia.
47	Mount Wellington	3,795	Van Diemen's Land.
48	Forest Hill	3,776	New South Wales.
49	Mount York	3,292	....
50	Mount Exmouth	3,000	....
51	King's Table-land	2,827	....
52	Sugar Loaf	2,527	....
53	Chaisgour	2,400	Vindhya Mountains, Ind.
54	Mount St Paul's	2,400	Van Diemen's Land.
55	Carmel	2,160	Syria.
56	Tabor	1,950	....

AFRICA.

1	Mountains of Geesh	15,000	Gojam, Abyssinia.
2	Mountains of Amid	13,000	....
3	Cameroons	13,000	Biafra.
4	Peak	12,236	Teneriffe.
5	Lamalmon	11,400	Samen Mountains, Abyssinia.
6	Miltsin	11,200	Marocco.
7	Clarence Peak	10,655	Fernando Po.
8	Nieuveldt	10,000	Beaufort, Cape of Good Hope.
9	Compassberg	10,000	Graffreynet, ditto.
10	Volcano	7,884	Fogo.